7/26/16

Dia[...]
my beautiful
babby daughter
I put God's Blessings
around you and
cover you with the
Blood of Jesus,
No weapon formed against
you will prosper.
Good health, happiness
and a good life will
always be...... Mom

LEADERSHIP

DEVOTIONS

Cultivating a Leader's Heart

Edited and selected by David Goetz
and the editors of Christianity Today International

TYNDALE HOUSE PUBLISHERS, INC.
WHEATON, ILLINOIS

Visit Tyndale's exciting Web site at www.tyndale.com

Leadership Devotions: Cultivating a Leader's Heart

This book was developed by Leadership Resources of Christianity Today International.

Designed by Melinda Schumacher

Edited by Susan Taylor

Library of Congress Cataloging-in-Publication Data

Printed in the United States of America

07	06	05	04	03	02	01
7	6	5	4	3	2	1

⬎CONTENTS

Introduction

AMBITION: 1. Ambition Crippler   1

   2. Whatever God Wants   5

ANGER: 3. Anger without Sin   9

APATHY: 4. Deciding to Decide   13

CALLING: 5. Leadership Lessons from *The Prince of Egypt*   17

CHARACTER: 6. Beyond the Packaging   21

   7. Unhappy? Maybe That's Good!   25

COMMITMENT: 8. Loving the Game When You're Losing   29

COURAGE: 9. Dashes of Courage   33

   10. Everyday Boldness   37

   11. Stepping into Something Frightening   41

CYNICISM: 12. The Cynic Within   45

   13. Cynicism or Realism?   49

DESIRE FOR GOD: 14. The Drink in the Desert   53

   15. No Stupid Questions   57

DISCONTENT: 16. Content with Enough   61

	17. Have You Been "Discovered"?	65
EGO:	18. The Unholy Trinity: Me, Myself, and I	69
GOD'S DISCIPLINE:	19. Telling Secrets	73
GOD'S FAITHFULNESS:	20. God in the In-Between	77
GOD'S GOODNESS:	21. When Leadership Hurts	81
GOD'S LOVE:	22. The Myth of Hard Work	85
	23. Getting out of the Way	89
	24. Love Overcomes All Fear	93
GOD'S PRESENCE:	25. When God Gives Us a Push	97
GOD'S TRANSCENDENCE:	26. What Is God Like?	101
GOD'S WORK IN US:	27. Your Words Came Out	105
GOD'S WORTHINESS:	28. Feet on Earth, Head in Heaven	109
GRACE:	29. Singled Out	113
	30. Can We Despise God's Grace?	117
HUMILITY:	31. True Greatness	121
IDENTITY:	32. Bringing Your Identity to Work	125
INTEGRITY:	33. Never Say Never	129
	34. Sir Paul Goes to the Palace	133
	35. The "God Compartment"	137

JOY: 36. Hints of Heaven 141

37. The Roots of a Joyful Spirit 145

LORDSHIP OF CHRIST: 38. The Difference between Profit and Prosperity 149

LOVE FOR GOD: 39. One Surpassing Love 153

MATERIALISM: 40. A Tale of Two Tables 157

PEACE: 41. Greater Than Our Accomplishments 161

PERSEVERANCE: 42. The God Who Perseveres 165

43. The Warehouse with Wings 169

PERSISTENCE: 44. Can We Change God's Mind? 173

PRIDE: 45. What You Don't See Can Hurt You 177

PURPOSE: 46. What's in the Box? 181

SELF-ACCEPTANCE: 47. "I Am What I Am" 185

SELF-INVENTORY: 48. Habit Tracking 189

SPIRITUAL MATURITY: 49. The Best Is Yet to Come 193

SPIRITUAL WARFARE: 50. Satan's a Bear 197

STRESS: 51. An Unseen Enemy 201

TRANSFORMATION: 52. Lifelong Learner 205

Contributors 209

Index of Topics 215

Index of Scripture References 221

Appendix 223

What is a leader? We could answer that question in a variety of ways. A very basic definition would be "A leader is someone who has followers." A slightly broader definition may be "A leader is someone who accepts responsibility for others." Some people would consider leaders those who simply have the ability to hide their panic from others!

Former Dallas Cowboys coach Tom Landry had one of the most intriguing definitions: "Leadership is getting people to do what they don't want to do so they can become what they've always wanted to be." It's easy to envision football coaches compelling athletes to do what they don't want to do (lift weights, run sprints, practice drill after endless drill) so they can become what they've always wanted to be (champions). You can also envision Christian leaders getting those in their spheres of influence to do what they might not want to do (practicing spiritual disciplines, selflessly giving of themselves) in order that they can become what they've always wanted to be (mature, complete, and Christlike). It seems obvious that compelling people to do what they don't want to do doesn't necessarily make a leader popular. But leading isn't about becoming popular. It's about accomplishing something worthwhile.

Jesus Christ pointed out the most important aspect of Christian leadership, and it is a great paradox: "Whoever wants to be a leader among you must be your servant" (Matt. 20:26). In other words, you can't be a good leader unless you're a good follower.

This book offers fifty-two devotions to help Christian leaders—not just pastors and teachers but those who exercise leadership in business, education, medicine, home and family, and other arenas—become better followers of Christ. These devotions, written by Christian leaders from a variety of backgrounds and compiled by the editors of *Leadership* journal, will help you consider how you can follow Christ willingly and well.

How can you get the most out of this book?

The book is arranged topically; that is, each devotion relates to a particular theme. Of course, you may choose to read through the book in order, one devotion at a time; you might even decide to read one devotion each week for a year. But you can also use the **topical index** in the back of the book to help you locate devotions that relate to a specific challenge you are facing in your role as a leader. The devotions in this book focus on internal aspects of leadership, on building and cultivating the inner character necessary in order to be an effective Christian leader. For example, the leader of a board of deacons could choose a devotion that deals with an issue the board is facing—perhaps commitment or humility—and use it to open a deacons meeting. A parent or business professional might choose a devotion on stress or anger that applies to an issue in the home or workplace. The index lists each devotion under both a primary topic (the theme that is indicated at the beginning of each devotion) and also under secondary topics, giving the greatest possible applicability to each devotion. We've also included a **Scripture index** to enable readers to locate devotions that are based on a specific portion of Scripture.

All of us are leaders in one way or another. Whether

you have the opportunity to influence the lives of those in your family, your church, your neighborhood, or your workplace, this book can help you to be a more effective leader in the place where God has put you. Then, as you do what you may not immediately want to do, you'll be transformed into what you've always wanted to be—a leader through whom God can do great and mighty things.

Marshall Shelley
Vice President, Editorial
Christianity Today International

AMBITION

Ambition Crippler

Lord, please! Send someone else.
EXODUS 4:13

THE first step on the road to success begins inside our heads. Until we grapple with our past failures and conquer our sense of inadequacy, we will never be able to handle success. But once we get the negative past out of our heads, we're able to journey toward a meaningful, fulfilling life.

Many typical motivational speeches—even sermons—skip this important mental step. But the negative, dream-crushing defeats in our past can drown out positive, faith-building talk. Our disappointments and failures can corrode our dreams for the future. Sure, we want to make a difference with our lives. But before we can develop a healthy ambition and a passion for God's purpose for us, before we can set our sights on God-honoring, God-pleasing success, we've got to deal with the baggage of our humanity.

When Moses was young, he made a huge mistake. He tried to take hold of his destiny and accomplish something great for God. But his timing and his methods were off, and he failed miserably. With a dead Egyptian buried in the sand and a price on Moses' head, he retreated to the backside of the desert. As Moses watched the sheep and replayed his mistakes in his head for forty years, he allowed his dreams to wither away.

Still carrying the shame and disgrace of his past, Moses wasn't ready to volunteer when God called him at the burning bush. He had no more ambition to do anything great for God—no passion for significant success. In fact, as God urged Moses to see the possibilities, Moses protested repeatedly.

"Who am I?" he asked (Exod. 3:11). He had lost the advantage of being raised in Pharaoh's household. Now he was merely an unknown, insignificant shepherd.

"What should I tell them?" he asked (v. 13). Moses couldn't imagine himself back in Pharaoh's courts, much less debating successfully with the most powerful leader in his world.

But in spite of his protests, feelings of inadequacy, and past failures, this insignificant, hypercautious, stuttering shepherd without a message finally bowed to the call and will of God. And with God's help, Moses became a leader for all time.

—Richard Doebler

REFLECTION

What events or people in my past have crippled my ambitions and potential to do something great for God? What will it take for me to become daring enough to be a success for God?

PRAYER

It's far too easy, Lord, to see nothing but my shortcomings and miss the sight of your long arm of grace that can help me successfully fulfill your call.

"When you begin thinking you really are number one, that's when you begin to go nowhere."

—Stevie Wonder, entertainer

AMBITION

Whatever God Wants

*I once thought all these things
were so very important, but now I
consider them worthless because of
what Christ has done. Yes,
everything else is worthless when
compared with the priceless gain
of knowing Christ Jesus my Lord.
I have discarded everything else,
counting it all as garbage, so that
I may have Christ.*

PHILIPPIANS 3:7-8

IT IS ironic that I, who had little ambition, gained such influence while others, who would kill to have such influence, may still be seeking it. But I don't think you necessarily find something by going directly at it.

When we were learning to spot airplanes in the dark, the navy taught us that the center part of our eyes are blind at night. If you try to look directly at where the sound of the plane is coming from at night, you never will see the plane. If you look to the right or the left of where you hear the sound, you'll see the plane out of the part of your eye that isn't night-blind. Ambition is like that.

People who pursue ambitious goals often are some of the most frustrated people in the world. And those who have succeeded oftentimes have been ruthless in their attempts to achieve it and have left bodies scattered over the landscape.

Those who pursued meaningful service rather than direct ambition, however, often reached their goals. For every one of the achievers—even the honest ones—there is an enormous number of people who years ago offered themselves for ministry and have never come close to achieving their goals. So we have to offer ourselves to God to do whatever *he* wants us to do and let the personal ambition go by the way.

—Richard Nelson Bolles

REFLECTION

Can I accomplish something for my business or my church without caring whether I get the credit?

PRAYER

Help me to be ambitious in the right way, Lord—not seeking my own success, but in seeking your honor and glory.

"So many missionaries, intent on doing something, forget that God's main work is to make something of them."

—Jim Elliot, martyred twentieth-century missionary

3

ANGER

Anger without Sin

A fool gives full vent to anger, but a wise person quietly holds it back. . . . A hot-tempered person starts fights and gets into all kinds of sin.

PROVERBS 29:11, 22

LOTS of people have the power to hurt or frustrate me. But whether or not I express my anger when they do is my choice. People don't "make me" angry; I allow myself to express my anger. No one else can make me respond aggressively or inappropriately when I feel anger. It often seems just the opposite because my response to feeling anger has become so routine that it seems "automatic." It feels as if the person or event triggered my anger and *caused* my response.

The truth is, so many of my responses to anger result from learned behavior. I learned it long ago, from people I grew up around. And I learned it so informally that I was not even aware of it.

Tommy Bolt has been described as the angriest golfer in the history of a game that has stimulated the secretion of more bile than any other single human activity outside of war and denominational meetings. One (possibly apocryphal) story recalls a time when he was giving a group lesson on how to hit a ball out of a sand trap.

Calling his eleven-year-old son over, he said, "Show the people what you've learned from your father when your shot lands in the sand." The boy picked up a wedge and threw it as high and as far as he could.

Anger is an inescapable fact of life. But the *experience* of anger is different from the *expression* of anger. What I do with my anger, how I express it and manage it, is another matter. The good news is that what we have learned we can also unlearn. It is possible for me to manage my anger in a God-honoring way: to be angry and not sin.

—John Ortberg

REFLECTION

How would my colleagues or spouse say I handle my anger?

PRAYER

God of peace and wisdom, give me a perspective that will help keep me from anger, and when I do get angry, give me the discernment to manage it in ways that will honor you and not hurt others needlessly.

"We need not 'sin that grace may abound.' We are sinners and need only to confess that grace may abound."

—C. FitzSimons Allison, retired Episcopal bishop and theologian

4

APATHY

Deciding to Decide

Always be full of joy in the Lord. I say it again—rejoice! Let everyone see that you are considerate in all you do. Remember, the Lord is coming soon.

Don't worry about anything; instead, pray about everything. Tell God what you need, and thank him for all he has done. If you do this, you will experience God's peace, which is far more wonderful than the human mind can understand. His peace will guard your hearts and minds as you live in Christ Jesus.

PHILIPPIANS 4:4-7

DURING his freshman year at Yale University, William Borden, the great missionary, wrote a prayer in his journal: "Lord Jesus, I take hands off as far as my life is concerned. I put thee on the throne of my heart. Change, cleanse, use me as thou shalt choose. I take the full power of thy Holy Spirit. I thank thee."

This faith changed Borden's life and set in motion a shift of direction that had a profound effect upon his student years at Yale and Princeton Theological Seminary and in his brief career as a missionary to Egypt. Borden died in Cairo of cerebral meningitis at the age of twenty-five; his life was short but full. His commitment to Jesus Christ and the world missionary mandate of the gospel continues to challenge those who know his story.

Borden's journal entry suggests the narrow and fragile dividing line that marks the difference between active commitment to life on the one hand and apathy toward life on the other. In both, we make a choice that could be described by Borden's words as a freshman: "I take hands off."

It is remarkable that the same brief sentence—"I take hands off"—could be the key opening thought for motivated action on the one side and demotivation from all action on the other. How can this be true? In both instances we "take hands off" when we realize the limitations of human power; in both instances we become disillusioned with human achievement and success; in both instances we feel a disappointment with people who fall short of our expectations. Nevertheless, what we do with these feelings of disappointment, inadequacy, or fatigue makes all the difference between discipleship and apathy.

Borden came to this moment as a young man. He knew himself well enough not to place himself at the center of his life; he also knew too well the inadequacy of the people and institutions around him and the futility of enthroning in his heart the church, Yale, or any idealistic program. What Borden did instead was to decide in favor of Jesus Christ as the living center for his life. He chose to be available to live under Christ's will, and he claimed the assurance of the Holy Spirit. This act of commitment to life in Christ made all the difference.

Apathy, by contrast, institutionalizes disappointment. The soul withdraws from all effort at discovery and eventually decides to stop deciding. This is what *apathy* means: "away from pathos"— away from suffering or any intense experience.

Is there a cure? Yes. It happens in stages for most people, but sooner or later it requires us to join up with the rest of the human race and finally demands that we, as William Borden did, decide to decide. It finally draws us into the rich colors of human feeling where the rewards are better than the possible dangers. Best of all, the cure draws us into fellowship with the nonapathetic Lord of life.

—Earl F. Palmer

15

REFLECTION

What would it mean for me to "take hands off"?

PRAYER

Lord Jesus, I thank you that your safe and strong hands surround my life today. I begin this prayer trusting in those good hands.

"If we are going to wait until every possible hindrance has been removed before we do a work for the Lord, we will never attempt to do anything."

—T. J. Bach

5

CALLING

Leadership Lessons from The Prince of Egypt

Moses protested again, "Look, they won't believe me! They won't do what I tell them. They'll just say, 'The Lord never appeared to you.'" Then the Lord asked him, "What do you have there in your hand?"

EXODUS 4:1-2

BEFORE the movie *The Prince of Egypt* was released, I was invited to preview the film for DreamWorks Studios. It was a thrill to be a part of this project, but on top of the excitement of the moment, God spoke to me during that animated film on the life of Moses. It happened during Moses' encounter with the burning bush, when he was arguing with the Lord about why he couldn't lead God's people out of Egypt. Moses felt utterly unqualified to lead anyone out of anywhere. After a couple of rounds of debate, God won by asking Moses a simple question: "What is in your hand?" Moses was holding a shepherd's staff, something he had been using for forty years as he herded sheep in the desert.

When God calls us into leadership, he usually starts with familiar tools, giving us a ministry that looks a lot like what we've been doing all along. The leadership role he calls us to may not even seem spiritual or significant at first glance.

This encounter between God and Moses is full of spiritual truths for leaders. Consider the following:

Faithfulness counts. God calls us to keep on doing what we've already been doing. Leaders are not necessarily more gifted than others, but they are less inclined to give up.

God seeks a willing attitude in us. Scripture reveals Moses' great reluctance to assume the role of deliverer of Israel, but in spite of his fears he obeyed the call of God upon his life.

God's power comes upon an obedient heart. In Moses' eyes his staff appeared to be just an ordinary staff, but in the hand of God it became something powerful and even life changing. From these verses on, Moses' staff was central as God guided Israel out of bondage. Each time an account mentions the staff, God is saying, in effect, "The common becomes significant when my power comes upon it."

God uses preparation. What we've *been* doing is preparation for what we *will* be doing. As the film showed, Moses—born an Israelite, raised an Egyptian, reunited with his captive people—was uniquely qualified, through his life and preparation, to lead his people out of bondage. In the economy of God, there is no wasted time.

—Steve Sjogren

REFLECTION

What is "in my hand" that God might anoint for service?

PRAYER

Lord, help me recognize that great opportunity isn't always something distant and "out there"—it may be right in front of me. Then, gracious Father, equip me with the courage and obedient spirit to act on those opportunities.

"Destiny is not a matter of chance; it is a matter of choice."

—William Jennings Bryan, American lawyer and politician

CHARACTER

Beyond the Packaging

*Some say, "Don't worry about
Paul. His letters are demanding
and forceful, but in person he is
weak, and his speeches are really
bad!" . . . I may not be a trained
speaker, but I know what I am
talking about. I think you realize
this by now, for we have proved it
again and again.*

2 CORINTHIANS 10:10; 11:6

RECENTLY I heard a missionary speaker, a woman who had served in the jungles of an equatorial country for almost forty years. She had a dowdy appearance; her hairdo was a little out of fashion, and she was not a particularly polished speaker. She shuffled her notes a few times and looked for a couple of quotes she'd lost in her notebook. She spoke quietly and humbly.

But I was invigorated and challenged. She told stories of how she and her husband took their small children into jungles where malaria was running rampant, where rivers were infested with crocodiles, where the monsoon rains came down, and where their tiny grass hut, up on twenty-foot pilings of bamboo, was shaking in the wind. The natives they were trying to reach were cannibals who practiced headhunting.

The fact that she wasn't a polished speaker made her stories, testimonies, and insights from God's Word all the more brilliant. They shined with a kind of unpolished glory. Her speaking was so un-man-made, so divine.

Unfortunately, not everyone in the audience was so impressed. It made me wonder, can we not rely on the Word of God or the Spirit of God to enable us to look at somebody through the light of his grace and see character, perseverance, self-control, self-discipline, a desire to obey?

—Joni Eareckson Tada

23

REFLECTION

How have I focused on my character development in recent years?

PRAYER

Lord, help me desire character more than charisma, a sound soul more than an impressive appearance.

"Common-looking people are the best in the world; that is the reason the Lord makes so many of them."

—Abraham Lincoln, sixteenth president of the United States

7

CHARACTER

Unhappy? Maybe That's Good!

*Long ago, even before he made the
world, God loved us and chose us
in Christ to be holy and without
fault in his eyes.*

EPHESIANS 1:4

SEMINAR titles rarely snare my attention. They're often too pat or too hyped. But in a planning meeting for a National Pastors Convention, this seminar title by Gary Thomas made my brainwaves quiver: "What If God Designed Marriage to Make Us More Holy Than Happy?"

I laughed out loud.

Nearly twenty years of marriage, full and rich marriage, have taught me that marriage by design exerts a relentless pressure on my self-absorption. It challenges me to serve, to sacrifice, to love—in short, to grow up. Martin Luther called marriage "The School of Character."

Contrary to hundreds of Hollywood romance movies, marriage is not primarily designed to make us happy. God is not primarily interested in our happiness but in something deeper and more lasting: our holiness. God is so interested in our long-term happiness—our eternal joy, which only holiness leads to—that he reserves the right to sacrifice our short-term happiness to ensure that we receive it.

I then applied Gary Thomas's concept to Christian leadership: "What if God designed leadership to make us more holy than happy?"

People who have never been leaders sometimes spin romantic fantasies about the glory and attention that come with the job. Luther once quipped that

God uses ambition to compel us to office. Apparently God uses our self-directed desires to move us to a place where he can teach us the hard lesson of serving others. For leadership, like marriage, is a School of Character. It means getting up early for prayer meetings. Staying up late for board meetings. Being criticized. Trying to do work without enough money, enough people, enough key leaders.

We may, especially on Mondays, when our adrenaline is depleted, contemplate quitting. But it is at this precise painful moment that we are where God wants us. Through these chiseling experiences, God sculpts our character. We thought becoming a leader would bring excitement, growth, results—that it would make us happy (all while we're serving God, of course).

But God is after something more valuable: to make us holy. He wants the soft, precious gold in the heart of the mountain, and he will move cartloads of rubble to get to it. God is not afraid to use criticism, discouragement, and limitation to blast away the hardened rock.

Are you discouraged about the difficulties of Christian leadership? They don't necessarily mean you're doing something wrong. They may mean that God is doing something right. He's making you holy.

—Kevin A. Miller

REFLECTION

In what ways is God making me holy through the difficulties I encounter as a leader?

PRAYER

Lord, as you chip away at those things that hinder holiness in my life, help me to remember that your goal is to produce a life that shines like gold.

"God is more concerned about our character than our comfort. His goal is not to pamper us physically but to perfect us spiritually."

—Paul W. Powell, author

8

COMMITMENT

Loving the Game When You're Losing

A final word: Be strong with the Lord's mighty power.

<small>EPHESIANS 6:10</small>

ERNIE Banks, the Chicago Cubs Hall of
Famer, is known not only for his accomplishments as a player but also for what he didn't
accomplish. Even though Banks was one of the
greatest players of his era and had a long and productive career, he never played in a World Series
or a play-off game. While Banks delighted Cubs
fans with his glove and his bat, his team became
permanent residents of the National League cellar. Yet Banks played with the intensity of a
champion, year in and year out. Recently in a
radio interview he was asked how he could play at
a peak level when there was little or no hope of
playing in a World Series. He responded with a
powerful statement: "You have to love the game
itself and not love yourself in the game." Banks
went on to explain that he loved the game of
baseball so much that he had to give his best
effort in every game.

It's easy to love the game when we're winning
and being recognized. When the company is setting sales records, when the church is packed,
when others are recognizing our achievements, it's
easy to strive for excellence and have passion for
the good and the godly. Yet in the years or the
seasons of life when there are no awards, no
bonuses, and little tangible success, it is tempting

to allow the warmth of our spiritual passion to drop below body temperature. But God calls us to be steadfast in our spiritual passion every day, even when we feel like losers.

The apostle Paul's admonition to be strong is followed by his instruction to put on the whole armor of God. Changing Paul's metaphor from a battlefield setting to a ballpark, a loose paraphrase of this would be, "Be strong, and put on the uniform of champion every day!"

—Gary Fenton

31

REFLECTION

Do I exhibit my spiritual passion even when there is no prospect of immediate reward?

PRAYER

Lord, give me a passion for your kingdom every day—not just on the days I am perceived as a winner.

"If the team wins, we all had a good year; if we don't win, then it doesn't matter who had a good year."

—Paul O'Neill, 1994 American League
batting champion

32

9

COURAGE

Dashes of Courage

*If you make the Lord your refuge,
if you make the Most High your
shelter, no evil will conquer you;
no plague will come near your
dwelling. For he orders his angels
to protect you wherever you go.*
PSALM 91:9-11

IN THE early 1500s two radical ideas crystallized in the mind of a university professor in the backwater town of Wittenberg, Germany: People are saved by faith (not by human effort), and Scripture (not the church) is the test of truth. These ideas seemed radically subversive to the authorities of the day, so the pope kicked the professor, Martin Luther, out of the church, and Charles V, the Holy Roman Emperor, ordered the "heretic" to appear before him.

Luther relished the idea of arguing his views before Charles, so he agreed to appear at Worms, Germany, in April 1521. Charles V sat on a dais, flanked by his advisers and representatives of Rome, and all around were his Spanish troops decked out in their parade best. The hall was filled with the politically powerful—bishops, princes, and representatives of the great cities. In the midst of this impressive assembly stood a table holding a pile of books.

An official asked Luther if had he written these books, and if so, was there a part of them he would now choose to recant? Luther was stunned. There would be no debate or hearing. His judges had already made their decision. In a voice that could barely be heard, Luther replied, "The books are all mine, and I have written more." To the second question, he answered, "This touches God and his Word. This affects the salvation of souls. I beg you, give me time." He was given one day, which he spent in turmoil over what he should do.

His life was now on the line.

The next evening the room was jammed with dignitaries, and as torches flickered, the same questions were again put to Luther. He began a short speech that was interrupted by his examiner, who rebuked the professor: "You must give a simple, clear, proper answer to the question: Will you recant or not?"

Luther's reply is now famous: "Unless I can be instructed with evidence from the Holy Scriptures . . . I cannot and will not recant." Knowing he could be arrested or killed for his answer, he concluded, "Here I stand. I can do no other. God help me. Amen."

It was a defining moment in history, but not for reasons we often might think. Luther is rightly honored today as the man who rediscovered grace and faith and the authority of Scripture. But it took more than faith or theological insight to make the Reformation. At just the right moment, it took a dash of courage.

—Mark Galli

35

REFLECTION

Where in my life—at work, at home, in the community—am I being called to courageously speak the truth?

PRAYER

Lord, help me to know when I should stand up for you, as well as how I should do it.

"Never for the sake of peace and quiet, deny your own experience or convictions."

> —Dag Hammarskjöld, second secretary-general of the United Nations (1905–1961)

10

COURAGE

Everyday Boldness

The king asked, "Well, how can I help you?"

With a prayer to the God of heaven, I replied, "If it please Your Majesty and if you are pleased with me, your servant, send me to Judah to rebuild the city where my ancestors are buried."

NEHEMIAH 2:4-5

A N IMPORTANT leader in our church told me that his work schedule had stretched him to the limit and he didn't know what to do about his church commitments. In these situations my default mode is to cut a person some slack. "Why don't we relieve you of your responsibility for a time," I'll usually say, "and you tell me when you're ready to serve again." Sometimes that is the right course, but I didn't think so in this case. I felt he needed to cut back on his work schedule (which he himself had set) rather than curtail his church involvement.

I told him I would pray and get back to him. Prayer only reinforced my view, and at that point I faced a decision. I knew that challenging him to sacrifice for Christ in this manner posed a big risk. He might misconstrue my appeal as an inconsiderate effort to exploit him and consequently abandon both his ministry and the church and leave us in dire straits. I decided, however, that I had to push through that wall of uncertainty and risk and say what I thought God wanted me to say to him.

I am thankful that he received my words well and continued in ministry.

Every day faithful leaders face hazardous moments, large and small. Such moments always

require courage if we are to give optimum leadership for the Lord's sake.

Nehemiah faced one of these gut-check
moments. As a captive in a foreign land he was
cupbearer to the king. He wanted to return home
and help his fellow Israelites, but he knew that
bringing up such a request to the king, who had
the power of life and death, would be to take his
life in his hands. "I was badly frightened," says
Nehemiah, but he goes on boldly to present his
request (see Neh. 2:1-8). In order to lead God's
people, Nehemiah had to press through danger.

Courage is not something leaders need every
now and then at a ministry crossroads such as a
building program. No, leaders of integrity need
courage every day as we face decisions, meetings,
and challenges that have the potential for loss and
pain. We risk emotional pain, ministry problems,
relationships, reputation, money, time, failure.
We are tempted to play it safe.

But we build our leadership and ministry on doz-
ens and hundreds of daily steps of courage: confront-
ing a halfhearted staffer, speaking our vision, making
a commitment, reading a critical letter, evaluating
our ministry's progress. These are the decisive
moments that define a courageous ministry.

—Craig Brian Larson

REFLECTION

In what hazardous situations have I been most tempted to "wimp out"? Do I have a lot to lose, or have I already given everything to the Lord? Which steps of courage do I find the most faith for, and why?

PRAYER

Father, when Christ lived on earth, he spoke words that were difficult for people to hear, and he was often misunderstood and rejected. Yet he continued to speak your truth and did the work you gave him to do in order to accomplish your purpose. Give me the courage to follow in his footsteps.

"Life shrinks or expands in proportion to one's courage."

—Anaïs Nin, American author

11

COURAGE

Stepping into Something Frightening

They will reply, "Lord, when did we ever see you hungry or thirsty or a stranger or naked or sick or in prison, and not help you?" And he will answer, "I assure you, when you refused to help the least of these my brothers and sisters, you were refusing to help me." And they will go away into eternal punishment, but the righteous will go into eternal life.
MATTHEW 25:44-46

ALL sorts of things get in the way of doing what we're called to do. Sometimes it's sloth; sometimes we simply get distracted. But often it's fear that stands in the way. And sometimes the only way to conquer fear is, as the commercial says, to "just do it."

In the early 1800s English prisons were pits of indecency and brutality. In the the women's division at Newgate Prison in London, for example, women awaiting trial for stealing apples were crammed into the same cell as women who had been convicted of murder or forgery (which was also a capital crime).

Eating, sleeping, and defecating all took place in the same confined area. Women begged or stole to get clothes, alcohol, and food. Many became despondent in such conditions and sat around in a drunken stupor, stark naked. Some even starved to death.

In short, it was no place for a lady, especially a seemingly delicate woman such as Elizabeth Fry.

Fry, the daughter of an English banker, married at age twenty into another wealthy family. Children came quickly, one on top of another, and eventually numbered eleven in all. Fry spent her days caring for her children and entertaining people of high society. Yet years earlier she had sensed a call to work on behalf of the downtrodden. While still a young bride and mother, she gave medicine and clothes to the homeless and helped establish a school for nurses. And at age thirty-three she found the courage to step inside London's Newgate Prison and begin visiting female prisoners. Friends and prison officials warned her about the risk of both the disease and the violence to which she was exposing herself, but she waved aside the warnings and kept visiting.

Soon visiting wasn't enough. She taught female prisoners basic hygiene, as well as sewing and quilting. She read the Bible to inmates and intervened for women on death row.

43

To nineteenth-century observers, Fry's efforts produced a miracle: Many of the reportedly wild and shifty inmates became, under her care, orderly, disciplined, and devout. Mayors and sheriffs from the surrounding regions (and later from other European countries) visited Newgate and began initiating reforms in their own jails and prisons.

Today Elizabeth Fry is remembered as a pioneer in prison reform. And yet the only thing that separated her from many others of her day was her willingness to step into a frightening environment to see what she could do.

—Mark Galli

REFLECTION

Am I not doing something that God is calling me to do mainly because I'm afraid?

PRAYER

Lord, fill me with a sense of your presence and power so that I might do what you've called me to do, even when I'm afraid.

"Courage is resistance to fear, mastery of fear, not absence of fear."

—Mark Twain, American author

12

CYNICISM

The Cynic Within

*Everything is so weary and
tiresome! No matter how much
we see, we are never satisfied. No
matter how much we hear, we are
not content.*

ECCLESIASTES 1:8

A WORD of kindness and a loaded revolver will get you a lot more than a word of kindness alone." Thus thinks the cynic.

The cynic flatters himself or herself a hard-eyed realist, a down-to-earth, unfazed, practical person of experience—especially in comparison with "the idiots who maintain some kind of fool hope or optimism." The cynic has been there, done that, and been disappointed. Won't do that again—no way! Won't feel that way again—not on your life! Won't be tricked into hope—too street-smart for that. The cynic has learned that when the person with experience meets the person with money, the one with experience usually ends up with the money, and the one with money ends up with experience.

The cynic pretty much knows it all—if "knowing it all" were confined to this side of the sun. "Under the sun," all is vanity, we're told. "Under the sun," all things are wearisome, faded, dull, meaningless, unfulfilling. This side of the eternal, cynicism definitely has its place, as the cynical preacher of Ecclesiastes knew all too well. Wine, women, and song; power, authority, and accomplishments; wisdom, learning, and knowledge—all mean so very little if we are only to die and fade into forgotten nothingness. What good is anything—from magnificent accomplishment to wretched excess—if it is only to be lost as a desiccated memory upon death?

Christian leaders, possessed of a wealth of experience and knowledge, can fall prey to cynical moods. We know a lot; we've heard it all; we've seen the good, the bad, and the ugly in people. Over time such knowledge and experience can corrode the soul, and a view that lofts no higher than the horizon is bound to float cynicism.

But not so a view that rises to the Creator, who is beyond the sun! Place God in the picture, and cynicism sinks into absurdity. Look beyond the sun into the providential heart of God, and cynicism becomes as out of place as gills in a desert.

The cynic has adapted to the apparent reality of godlessness. In a God-filled universe, however, cynicism is maladaptive behavior. Hope responds better to the realities of providence. Faith and courage spring from the awakening sensation of God's prevenient grace that greets us in the morning, having already bettered the day. Peace and an open, tender heart characterize the person who has been received, recategorized, and released to a noble task and a secure future.

Not cynicism! However trendy, however convenient, however natural it might seem to be a cynic, that wretched path has been overgrown by the lavish foliage of the Savior's love.

—James D. Berkley

47

REFLECTION

In what ways am I drawn toward the maladaptive behavior of cynicism in God's hope-filled kingdom, and how can I lessen that attraction?

PRAYER

God of hope, Giver of a good and perfect future, quench the cynic within me!

"History is an account, mostly false, of events, mostly unimportant, which are brought about by rulers, mostly knaves, and soldiers, mostly fools."

—Ambrose Bierce, nineteenth-century
American author

13

CYNICISM

Cynicism or Realism?

*When she saw King David
leaping and dancing before the
Lord, she was filled with contempt
for him.*

2 SAMUEL 6:16

THOSE who think too much can slip into cynicism by overanalyzing people and situations.

Michal, King David's wife, was a thinker and an analyzer. She understood political power. Growing up in the shadow of her father, King Saul, Michal had learned to be suspicious. King Saul, perhaps Israel's most paranoid ruler, had taught his daughter to distrust and fear others: If people say something nice, you'd better question their motives. They're probably out to take advantage of you, maybe even to take your place.

Observing her father, Michal saw how difficult it is to stay on top, ahead of all challengers. She learned that a leader should never let down his guard or risk being deceived. By watching her father, Michal learned to doubt the sincerity of others. She allowed suspicion and doubt to grow in her heart and poison her outlook on life.

On the day when the ark of the Lord was brought into the city, Michal's cynicism erupted. Celebration filled the air that day, and David was about to see his dream fulfilled. Unable to restrain his excitement, he enthusiastically joined in the festivities and "danced before the Lord with all his might, wearing a priestly tunic" (2 Sam. 6:14).

Watching the scene from a window above,

Michal was appalled at her husband's public display. She thought, *Where is the decorum and dignity befitting a king? Where is the royal pomp and ceremony?* Michal believed people would lose respect for a king who behaved in such a common manner. In a voice dripping with sarcasm, she cut into him: "How glorious the king of Israel looked today! He exposed himself to the servant girls like any indecent person might do!" (v. 20).

Michal couldn't understand David's trusting, freewheeling spirit. Cynics don't understand such people. They see themselves as realists and think of trusting, unguarded people as simple and naive. Michal thought David was too carefree and that his irresponsible actions could jeopardize his position. *Doesn't he care about guarding the dignity of his office?* she wondered. *Doesn't he care about opinion polls? Doesn't he care about the political fallout for his behavior?*

Cynicism caused Michal to despise David for what she perceived as his naïveté and careless disregard for political realities. Some would say that in turn, Michal's cynicism prevented Michal from achieving a fruitful and productive life (v. 23).

—Richard Doebler

REFLECTION

Do I sometimes overanalyze people's motives or question their sincerity? What's the difference between a cynical distrust of others and the ability to cultivate a healthy discernment?

PRAYER

Lord, teach me today to trust you more so that I can trust others more and be free of the suspicions and doubts that lead to a cynical spirit.

"The cynic is one who never sees a good quality in a man, and never fails to see a bad one."

—Henry Ward Beecher, nineteenth-century pastor

14

DESIRE FOR GOD

The Drink in the Desert

*As the deer pants for streams of
water, so I long for you, O God.*
PSALM 42:1

IN THE dog days of the sweltering summer when I was ten years old, my family drove across the Mojave Desert to go camping at the Grand Canyon. Our Chevrolet sedan had no air conditioning. The blacktop ahead of us softened in the heat, shimmering surrealistically.

Mom and Dad were up front, Dad driving; my three younger brothers and I were crammed into the backseat. A couple weeks earlier we had coerced a stray German shepherd-like mutt to follow us home. We begged Mom until she let us keep him, and we named him Bruno. Now Bruno was lying next to the back window, panting incessantly, his white fur floating around in the car and sticking to my skin. My fingers were so swollen with the heat that I couldn't remove a souvenir ring I'd bought. My tongue cleaved to the roof of my mouth.

That night at ten-thirty we pulled into Blythe, California, where the thermometer on the bank read ninety degrees. We sighted an A&W Root Beer sign and turned into the parking lot. I don't think I've ever tasted anything as good as the frosty mug of root beer I quaffed there.

In Psalm 42 the psalmist speaks of a longing for God so intense it's like a dry-mouthed thirst on a scorching day. He grieves the fact that he can't be at the temple in Jerusalem. Why is he estranged from his spiritual home? Perhaps he wrote from exile, cut off in Babylon from the place where he found God to be most authentically present.

Wherever he was, far from home, the psalmist cries out, "As the deer pants for streams of water, so I long for you, O God." Do we have that same thirst, that same intense desire for the presence of God?

The psalmist says we need to become aware of our deep thirst for the living God. God is to the soul what water is to the body, and our thirst bears witness to our need. When we tire of the aridity of our culture, when we despair over our own dryness, when we grow discouraged over the seeming distance of God, all we can do is cry out to God. That's a good place to begin, for God is the one who puts that thirst in us.

We were made to be satisfied with the Living Water. And if we recognize our thirst, we are blessed, because God is able to satisfy.

—Randal C. Working

REFLECTION

What makes me aware of my desire for God?
What helps me quench that thirst?

PRAYER

Lord, you who alone can satisfy, I long to come into
your presence.

*"In God's time and in God's way the desert will give
way to a land flowing with milk and honey. And as we
wait for that promised land of the soul, we can echo
the prayer of Bernard of Clairvaux, 'Oh my God, deep
calls unto deep (Ps. 42:7). The deep of my profound
misery calls to the deep of your infinite mercy.'"*

—Richard Foster, writer

15

DESIRE FOR GOD

No Stupid Questions

What are you looking for?
JOHN 1:38, NRSV

ONE day John the Baptist pointed to Jesus Christ and said, "Look, here is the Lamb of God." Two of John's disciples left him that day and immediately began to follow Jesus. When Jesus realized they were walking behind him, he turned and asked them, "What are you looking for?"

That is such a good question.

I can envision these two new disciples with their heads down, each nudging the other to answer Jesus' question. Finally, one of them says, "Teacher, where are you staying?"

The other guy must have put his face in his hands. *What a dumb answer! Why didn't he say that they were looking for truth, or maybe the kingdom of God?*

To be honest, most of the questions I ask God really aren't very profound either. I would love to impress God with my speculations about the inner dynamics of the Trinity, but I'm not up all night thinking about that. The things that keep me up at night are much more trivial.

Most of us don't really yearn for world peace. We think world peace is a good idea, but what we are deeply concerned about and think about continually are issues like losing weight or getting our teenagers to talk to us.

The disciple's question, "Teacher, where are you staying?" was not a serious or deep question. But what's fascinating is that Jesus took the question seriously and invited the two men to follow him home. There they stayed with him, probably talking about a lot of ordinary things. Apparently the conversation was so ordinary that John didn't bother recording it in his Gospel. I'm sure Jesus eventually talked about salvation, but he must have spent a lot of time fulfilling the disciples' ordinary yearnings before he could expose their longings for God.

The important thing is not what they discussed but with whom they were talking. There are no dumb questions with Jesus. There aren't any smart ones either. Frankly, it doesn't matter what we are looking for in life. If we turn the search into a prayer, Jesus will use it to reveal more of himself to us. And once we come to see who he is, the other questions will become less important. That means about halfway through our prayers, if we are paying attention, it should not be uncommon for us to say, "Now, what was I asking? I really can't remember."

—M. Craig Barnes

REFLECTION

Do your prayers focus on the things for which you are asking or on the one to whom you are speaking?

PRAYER

Keep me praying without ceasing, God, until I come to see that it is for you alone that I really yearn.

"He who prays fervently knows not whether he prays or not, for he is not thinking of the prayer which he makes, but of God, to whom he makes it."

—Francis de Sales, early seventeenth-century devotional writer

60

16

DISCONTENT

Content with Enough

*It's only the fruit from the tree at
the center of the garden that we
are not allowed to eat. God says
we must not eat it or even touch
it, or we will die.*

GENESIS 3:3

WHEN we think of "forbidden fruit," what usually comes to mind are things that are bad for us—alcohol, adultery, the corruption of wealth and power. But forbidden fruit may also signify something we've yearned for that God has chosen not to give us: the success just beyond our grasp, a dream we've chased most of our lives, a relationship with a particular person.

It's easy to obsess about this thing we don't and can't have—this forbidden tree standing in the midst of everything else God has given us. In fact, what we *don't* have can overshadow all our other gifts. And with this yearning comes sin, which is the choice to re-create our own lives after our own image of goodness. Along the way we may tell ourselves all sorts of lies, not the least of which is that we can be our own creators. Judging God's work in our lives to be too slow or too fast, too dull or too frightening, we reach for something more than we were ever created to have.

Significantly, when the serpent found Adam and Eve, they were standing by the forbidden tree. I wonder if, like us, they didn't spend a lot of time staring at that tree. There are so many trees that we can freely enjoy, but we fixate on the one that is missing.

Tragically, when we reach for that which is

beyond our created limits, we lose the Garden of Eden—often filled with a family, a job, and a life-style that really was good enough. In fact, it was more than good enough—it was paradise. But we didn't realize that until we lost it.

It's not that we should never dream or try to improve our lives. But we can, and should, resist the temptation to be consumed by our yearning.

—M. Craig Barnes

REFLECTION

What does the Bible mean when it tells us that God's grace is sufficient? Sufficient for what?

PRAYER

Oh, God of grace, give me the courage to confront the truth about my poor choices, and restore me to the paradise of knowing you.

"We are disgusted by the things that we desire, and we desire what disgusts us."

—Mario Cuomo, former governor of New York

17

DISCONTENT

Have You Been "Discovered"?

*Fight the good fight for what we
believe. Hold tightly to the eternal
life that God has given you, which
you have confessed so well before
many witnesses.*
1 TIMOTHY 6:12

WITH two kids under four, night school, and church responsibilities, I don't spend a lot of time on the couch in front of the TV, but I love *Behind the Music,* a VH1 program that narrates the behind-the-scenes stories of the rise and fall of rock stars. I've watched the *Behind the Music* stories of Led Zeppelin, Billy Joel, Mötley Crüe, Tina Turner, and a host of others. It's a kick to see what's happened to the bands I grew up with.

But I love the stories for another reason: The interviews with the stars are refreshingly candid. In most of the profiles there seems to be little spin control. Julian Lennon, son of legendary Beatle John Lennon, described the pain of growing up in a home where his father sang "All you need is love" in public but didn't show much love to his son in private.

The wretched-excess stories of *Behind the Music* are poignant reminders about the vain pursuit of fame, ambition, and success—the American Dream. If we achieve our dream, we're often left casting about for new directions. If we don't achieve it, our perceived inadequacy can motivate us wrongly for years.

A friend recently told me about the day he realized he would never be "discovered." He had served as a pastor for years with the notion that one day he would get a phone call from a large church in a nice suburb and his dreams would be fulfilled. When he was in his forties, my friend had heard that he was one of the candidates for a plum senior-pastor position in his denomination. But the church never called him, not even to ask for his résumé. My friend later learned that the church had filled the position. "It didn't hurt my ego to know I was not asked to be their pastor," he said, "but it was tough to swallow that, given all the hype, I wasn't even in the top twenty.

"After I learned of the decision, I returned to my study to finish the message for the midweek worship service. Humbled, I told myself I would rather be in the will of God than in my dream church. I grieved that I never had the opportunity to meet the committee. Then I looked at my ordination certificate hanging on the wall and saw the names of the ordination council—Tom, Roy, H. A., and Gerald—lay leaders, deacons, and bivocational ministers who had served in a rural county. I remembered their affirmation when they laid their hands on me and blessed me—and realized I had been discovered."

The best kind of satisfaction comes from discovering and living out the call God has placed on your life.

—Dave Goetz

REFLECTION

How would I feel if someone told me my professional life would plateau where it is right now?

PRAYER

God, you know that sometimes I secretly harbor dreams of being "discovered." I commit those dreams to you to use for your purposes. In the meantime, help me to understand what it means to be content where I am.

"When you get to the top of the mountain, your first inclination is not to jump for joy, but to look around."

—James Carville, political consultant

18

EGO

The Unholy Trinity: Me, Myself, and I

The sacrifice you want is a broken spirit. A broken and repentant heart, O God, you will not despise.

PSALM 51:17

ASHLEIGH Brilliant, that odd vestige of the seventies who scribbled his offbeat humor on hippie postcards, once penned: "All I ask of life is a constant and exaggerated sense of my own importance." People chortled at that observation thirty years ago. People absolutely live by it today.

Is egoism one of the greatest sins of Christian leaders, especially of those who are effective, successful, respected Christian leaders? Perhaps even of you? Our egos are a strange entity of proportion and moderation. Psychologically, a person with no ego would be a basket case without self-control or a concept of personal identity. Practically, a person with a deficient ego flounders in self-doubt, failure, and lack of confidence. On the other hand, we find a person who has an inflated sense of self-worth an insufferable blowhard, an egomaniac, a self-aggrandizing mass of arrogance. Every life needs some kind of balance between single-minded self-centeredness and excessive self-deprecation.

The famous rabbi Hillel wrote, "If I am not for myself, who will be for me? But, if I am for myself alone, what am I?" Rabbi Hillel, for all his wisdom, appears to be leaving out the most important factor: God. God always alters the ego scale. King David—rich, highly successful, and therefore, one who had every reason to develop a robust ego—eventually realized that next to God he was nothing! In fact, the most pleasing thing he could do for God was to declare his own absolute ego bankruptcy.

A broken ego won't ever hold enough air to become overly inflated. Next to God, no puny mortal ego dare claim hyperdimensions. We are the wearers of filthy rags next to God's splendor. We are the vessels made for destruction, apart from the Potter's grace. We are but dust and chaff. No, next to God, ego cannot inflate.

But because of God, we are fitted in regal finery. We are adopted as members of the royal family and destined for eternity. We are made just a little lower than God. Because of God, our personal significance becomes of staggering proportions. When we get that picture in our minds, an ego of proper dimensions ought to fit into place. We won't, as a Texan once said, be forever trying to put a ten-gallon hat on an eleven-gallon head. A superheated ego and a true sense of the lordship of Jesus Christ just don't fit in the same personality.

—James D. Berkley

REFLECTION

How can I acknowledge, celebrate, and take satisfaction in what God is doing in and through me without becoming or appearing egotistic?

PRAYER

Lord God, I give you the praise and glory for the good things you've placed in my life, and I ask you to break my arrogance in any areas of personal pride.

"The biggest addiction we have to overcome is to the human ego. Why? Because ego stands for Edging God Out."

—Kenneth Blanchard, popular author

19

GOD'S DISCIPLINE

Telling Secrets

David was now in serious trouble
because his men were very bitter
about losing their wives and
children, and they began to talk of
stoning him. But David found
strength in the Lord his God.
1 SAMUEL 30:6

EARL was a leader. This was evident at home, at work, in the community, and at church. If you wanted something done and someone to recruit followers, you got Earl. Grateful for the gifts God had given him, Earl found more significance at church than at work. However, beneath the smiling, confident exterior that Earl displayed in public, a dark anger lurked. The only people who saw it were those who experienced it—the members of his family. His wife and children lived in fear of Earl's outbursts of rage. He lived in constant fear that one day the public would know the private Earl. Then a chain of events occurred that threatened to force Earl to expose his sins.

David faced a similar situation in 1 Samuel 30. His disobedience to God and his lying to Achish led to a disastrous chain of occurrences. His city was destroyed, his family and those of his men were presumed lost, and his own men wanted to kill him. Just as God had used Samuel, a witch, and Philistines to confront Saul, he was using circumstances to confront David. Saul had responded foolishly and became God's enemy, but David responded wisely and found his strength in God. Therefore, God could help him.

When we open ourselves up to God, laying our

secrets and sins before him, submitting to his loving correction, we are forced to decide whom we trust—ourselves or God. God, like a loving parent, disciplines us for our good. Our choice is to respond in faith or attempt to hide from God.

Earl, like David, chose wisely. He dealt with his sin, and as a result God helped him. The Lord helped break the power of Earl's secret; God taught him how to handle shame and guilt; he provided spiritual siblings to minister to Earl; and he taught Earl to have complete trust in him. Earl learned that in God's kingdom no leader is as effective as a wounded leader.

—Paul Borden

REFLECTION

Are there areas in my life where the disparity between my public and private selves could prove destructive?

PRAYER

Lord, as the psalmist said, "You have searched me and you know me." And yet you still accept me! Help me to remember this bit of grace so that I might have the courage to live a life of integrity in which my private and public selves both live in your grace.

"People are like stained-glass windows. They sparkle and shine when the sun is out. But in the darkness, beauty is seen only if there is a light within."

—Anonymous

20

GOD'S FAITHFULNESS

God in the In-Between

*Teach me to do your will, for you
are my God. May your gracious
Spirit lead me forward on a firm
footing.*
PSALM 143:10

THE night before my wife, Mary Alice, was operated on for a brain tumor, I sat thinking as she slept, realizing this could be our last night together. I needed to hear a word from the mountain. It came from a surprising source: a young Elvis Presley singing gospel songs.

He opened with "Peace in the Valley." One line that especially hit me was "There will be peace in the valley for me." I was in the valley; I needed to realize God's peace. Then he sang "Precious Lord, take my hand. . . . I am tired, I am weak, I am worn." And I was. Then came the triumphant line from another song: "I know who holds tomorrow, / And I know who holds my hand." I responded with faith and said, "Hold on to the hope." Elvis next sang "Just a Closer Walk with Thee." My heart echoed, "I am weak, but thou art strong. . . . I'll be satisfied as long / As I walk, let me walk close to thee." I found in that holy moment of music the vitality of faith I needed, and it carried me through the operation.

Yet God also meets us on our mountaintops, when things are going well. My friend Bob is a successful New York executive who has made it big in Australia. Bob is an atheist. He surprised me, therefore, with his criticism of atheism, saying, "Fred, the worst thing about being an atheist is that when everything goes much better than I deserve, I have no one to thank. I wish I believed in God so I could thank him for my good fortune."

But does God also meet us on the level places? Bob's comment made me wonder, *Is God just for the extreme times of blessings?*

On the other hand, the secular press reported that the counselors sent into the schools following the terrible Littleton, Colorado, school tragedy were sitting idle while the students were crowding the churches, praying and sharing their grief with each other. I know their feelings and share them, but now the question is, Is God just for the tragedies in our lives?

Could Satan harm us any more than by getting us to relegate God to the extreme times of our lives? The extremes are temporary and pass away. The vast majority of our lives are spent in the ordinary, the unspectacular "humdrum" routine of living our day-to-day existence. Yet God assures us that he is forever faithful. His presence is constant, whether we are on the mountaintop, in the valley, or plodding along the long road across the plains.

—Fred Smith Sr.

REFLECTION

How can I sensitize myself to seeing God through the humdrum of my life?

PRAYER

God, it's another typical day—not much exciting, just more of the same. Yet I sense your presence, I seek your guiding hand, and I rejoice in spite of the routine simply because you have chosen me to be your child.

"My grandmother used to tell me that every boss is temporary, that every rainy day is temporary, that every hardship is temporary. She used to tell me, 'Son, every good-bye ain't gone. Just hold on—there's joy coming in the morning.'"

—James Melvin Washington, late pastor and author

21

GOD'S GOODNESS

When Leadership Hurts

*The Lord replied, "I will make all
my goodness pass before you, and I
will call out my name, 'the Lord,'
to you." . . . He passed in front of
Moses and said, "I am the Lord, I
am the Lord, the merciful and
gracious God. I am slow to anger
and rich in unfailing love and
faithfulness. I show this unfailing
love to many thousands by
forgiving every kind of sin and
rebellion."*

EXODUS 33:19; 34:6-7

SOME days it's really hard to be a Christian leader, especially if you have any contact with hurting people. I've listened in horror as an older man described through his tears how the sexual advances of a male relative stole the little boy in him. I've wept with a faithful wife who, when she heard that her husband was leaving her, was so distraught that she couldn't even stand up. Violence, selfishness, disease, senseless tragedy—the pain piles up like a multicar collision. On days like this it's hard not to question God's goodness. The little Sunday school chorus "God is so good, he's so good to me" just doesn't ring true when you've been around real life for a while.

Moses understood the heights-to-depths nature of leadership. From the literal peak experience of receiving the two tablets with God's instructions on Mount Sinai, he descended to discover a nation out of control, worshiping an idol and becoming a laughingstock to its enemies. For a while God even contemplated destroying Israel. But eventually, when Moses asked the Lord to show him his glory, God passed in front of him, defining his goodness.

He defined his goodness in terms of compassion—a word that in Hebrew is related to the term for womb and signifies the kind of love a mother has for her unborn baby growing inside her. God defined his goodness in terms of slowness to anger—the Hebrew literally says that God is "long of nose," which means it takes a long time for his face to flush in anger. He abounds in "loyal love"—affection for and faithfulness to his people. He is gracious and forgiving.

On a regular basis, leaders need to refresh their picture of God. If I look at God through the lens of circumstances, I can easily conclude that he's not good. But God calls his leaders to look at their circumstances through the lens of his goodness.

—Steve Mathewson

REFLECTION

How has God showed me his goodness during the past week? the past month? the past year?

PRAYER

God, you are kindness; you are patience; you are faithfulness; you are compassion; you are grace; you are love; you are good!

"That God is good is taught or implied in every page of the Bible and must be received as an article of faith as impregnable as the throne of God. It is a foundation stone for all sound thought about God and is necessary to moral sanity."

—A. W. Tozer, twentieth-century pastor and writer

84

22

GOD'S LOVE

The Myth of Hard Work

A voice from heaven said, "This is my beloved Son, and I am fully pleased with him."

MATTHEW 3:17

PEOPLE were coming to John to repent and be baptized. This baptism was different from Christian baptism. Its purpose was to wash away sin and allow the person to start over with a clean slate. Since people kept sinning, they had to keep coming back to be rebaptized—to start over and try to get their lives right. John's religion was not complicated. He claimed, "It is up to you to clean up your life and get right with God. If you do, you will be spared when judgment comes."

We don't quite get it, either—especially those of us who are hardworking and achievement oriented. We like John's message. Or at least we understand it. It's a religion that says, "Try harder. It's all up to you." That is the same religion we find at work and school, and maybe even at home. It's the same religion we may find, more subtly conveyed, at church. We like that message because it appeals to something heroic in us. We like to think that if we work hard enough, we will get life right.

So we understand why John was confused the day Jesus Christ showed up in the wilderness asking to be baptized. "Jesus, you haven't failed. Jesus, you're the standard we are trying to meet." But Jesus said his baptism was necessary "to fulfill all righteousness." In other words, this is the only way everyone will be made right—if he, the sin-less One and the Judge, comes to us who are lost in a sea of good intentions.

In his coming to be baptized, Jesus changed everything. When the Son of God identified himself with us in that way, the heavenly Father was so excited, he ripped back the skies. The Spirit of God descended like a dove, and a voice said, "This is my beloved Son, and I am fully pleased with him."

Nowhere in the Bible are we told that God is impressed by how hard someone is trying. Instead, what pleases God is that in Jesus Christ, God has found you. To be found in Christ means we can hear God saying, "You, too, are my son, my daughter, with whom I am pleased."

When we are baptized, we who follow Jesus do not try to wash away sins. That's hopeless, and we know it because we just keep sinning. We are baptized to identify ourselves with Jesus and to mark ourselves as a people who will live only by his loving grace—not by our own efforts or accomplishments.

—M. Craig Barnes

REFLECTION

How comfortable am I with the idea that I don't have to do anything to be loved by God?

PRAYER

Give me, Lord, the courage to accept the freedom offered in my baptism. For I know the only way to miss the future you have for me is to cling to the judgment of the past.

"Baptism points back to the work of God, and forward to the life of faith."

—J. Alec Motyer

GOD'S LOVE

Getting out of the Way

> The Lord is my shepherd; I have
> everything I need. He lets me rest
> in green meadows; he leads me
> beside peaceful streams. He renews
> my strength. He guides me along
> right paths, bringing honor to his
> name.
>
> PSALM 23:1-3

GOD the Almighty, who keeps the sky and stars from falling and the oceans from flooding the earth, is not content with simply spinning the planets. In Jesus Christ, God chooses to love us and offers to guide our lives.

For our part, however, we like to tell God exactly what to do in our lives: "If you really loved me, you would heal me . . . give me a new job . . . make my life more pleasant." When we do this, of course, we're just trying to use God to fulfill our own aspirations. Even if God did fulfill them, they wouldn't satisfy us as we hope they will. God loves us too much to be limited to our small dreams. That's because we were created for something better.

But that something better—a relationship of holiness with God—requires that we give up every other love, commitment, and dream. That's scary because we have no idea where God will take us or how he will care for us (or how we will live without all those things we've asked for). But he does promise to lead us into a place where love will conquer all our fears.

—M. Craig Barnes

91

REFLECTION

What is the one desire you need to let go of to better follow Jesus Christ?

PRAYER

Overwhelm me, oh, God, with so much of your perfect love, that it will cast out all of the fear that hinders me from following your Son, my only Savior, Jesus Christ. Amen.

"I believe the will of God prevails; without him all human reliance is vain; without the assistance of that Divine Being I cannot succeed; with that assistance I cannot fail."

—Abraham Lincoln, sixteenth president of the United States

24

GOD'S LOVE

Love Overcomes All Fear

*We know how much God loves us,
and we have put our trust in him.
God is love, and all who live in
love live in God, and God lives in
them. And as we live in God, our
love grows more perfect. So we
will not be afraid on the day of
judgment, but we can face him
with confidence because we are
like Christ here in this world.*

*Such love has no fear because
perfect love expels all fear.*

1 JOHN 4:16-18

WHEN I was a young child, my mother took me on a trip by plane. In those days airplanes weren't anything like they are today. We flew through a snowstorm, the wings froze up, and we made a somewhat difficult landing. We did walk away, but I was afraid of flying from that day forward. From the time I was five until I started consulting with churches twelve years ago, I boarded a plane only once.

When I first began consulting, I had to take a tranquilizer in order to get on an airplane, something I was not proud about. After a year or two of this nonsense I decided I had to do something, so I took flying lessons. I'll never forget the day my instructor said to me, "Pull over on the taxiway, and drop me off. It's time for you to solo." My heart practically left my body! But a year later I got my pilot's license, and my fear of flying was conquered.

What happened? My desire to follow God's call in my life cast out my fear of flying. I've been traveling 100,000-plus miles a year ever since.

I find that life is that way as well. As we grow in our understanding of God's love, we can overcome a world of fear. That's why the words of John, "Perfect love expels all fear," have a special meaning for me. It is really hard to be afraid when you know deep down that God really loves you.

As a consultant to churches and pastors, I have seen a lot of giving up lately. Things get so bad that church leaders are resigned to the death of a church; a pastor decides to retire early rather than retool; another pastor decides it's easier to do what people in the church want done—even if what they want isn't biblical—than it is to live with their wrath.

However, every time I see church leaders making a difference with their lives, it is because they are so in love with the God of Jesus Christ that they are driven by love and not fear.

The next time you are tempted to give in to the church bully, remember these words: *Perfect love expels all fear.*

—William "Bill" Easum

95

REFLECTION

Is God's love more real to me than my fears and anxieties? What would my life and work look like if I were to act on the assurance of that love regardless of possible consequences?

PRAYER

God, you know how fearful I am about
_____. Help me to see that only through your love and strength can I conquer that fear—and to act on that knowledge.

"Courage is being scared to death but saddling up anyway."

—John Wayne, actor

25

GOD'S PRESENCE

When God Gives Us a Push

*Yes, the Sovereign Lord is
coming in all his glorious power.
He will rule with awesome
strength. . . .
Who else has held the oceans
in his hand? Who has measured
off the heavens with his fingers?*

Isaiah 40:10-12

I USED to compete in gymnastics in all six men's events. In my earliest days on the still rings I was learning a move that involves swinging as fast as possible through the bottom and continuing right up into a handstand. At first I couldn't even get up into a shoulder stand, much less a handstand. To help me get a feel for the move, my coach stood alongside me, and as I swung through the bottom, he put his hand on my back and pushed hard. Suddenly I flew into a handstand! With my coach's hand on me I performed a move I could never do otherwise.

The prophet Isaiah wrote, "The Lord spoke to me with his strong hand upon me" (Isa. 8:11, NIV). In the sort of vivid word picture that Isaiah often uses, he describes God's powerful presence as being akin to having God place his hand on him. When Isaiah prophesied, it was like flying into a handstand on the rings.

With God's "hand" on him, Isaiah did things he could never do otherwise. Without the hand of God, Isaiah probably wrote wonderful poetry. With the hand of God, though, Isaiah wrote lines such as "He was pierced for our transgressions, he was crushed for our iniquities."

There is a great temptation in our work for the Lord. Most leaders have some degree of what seem like natural strengths: speaking or organizational ability, physical attractiveness or a winsome personality. The danger is that we can rely on ourselves rather than on the hand of the Lord, content to go without God's presence. The true test of our attitude is in our actions: If we minister without praying, without seeking God's presence and help, then no matter what we say to the contrary, deep down we think we can get by without God's hand upon us.

On the other hand, whatever our abilities, all leaders know what it's like to be in way over our heads. We know that without God's grace we are in big trouble. At those times we can rely on the hand of the Lord, who is always with us.

In gymnastics a coach's helping hand is temporary; not so with God's. God wants leaders to do everything with him because leaders can do nothing of kingdom value on their own. God wants us to do everything with his strong hand on us.

Never be content to lead others without God's presence. Not only your own spiritual welfare but the spiritual welfare of others depends on it.

—Craig Brian Larson

REFLECTION

How do I know when I have fallen into relying on myself instead of on the Lord? When have I experienced God's hand on me in leadership? What would need to change for me to be more consciously dependent on God's presence as I lead?

PRAYER

Almighty God, as you had your hand on Isaiah and David and Ruth and Abraham and Sarah, as you had your hand on Paul and Peter and Mary and Martha, so rest your hand on me.

"Peace is not the absence of trouble. Peace is the presence of God."

—Unknown

26

GOD'S TRANSCENDENCE

What Is God Like?

"My thoughts are completely different from yours," says the Lord. "And my ways are far beyond anything you could imagine. For just as the heavens are higher than the earth, so are my ways higher than your ways and my thoughts higher than your thoughts."

ISAIAH 55:8-9

ANY of us are tempted to respond, "Like us." We so can overemphasize the God who is so involved with our lives that he begins to look like us, and in so doing, we diminish his complete holiness and transcendence. A friend said to me, "All our sins can be classified under three categories: deifying of man, humanizing of God, and minimizing of sin." This insight has been very helpful for me in evaluating my concepts of God.

We humanize God when we think he is motivated in the same ways humans are. For example, we subconsciously feel more secure if we believe God needs us rather than believe that he only loves us. This thinking implies that God uses us to satisfy his selfish need. Since we strive to satisfy *our* needs and value those people and things that fulfill our needs, we reason that God appreciates and rewards our satisfying his needs.

But God has no needs because God is sovereign. God loves us; he doesn't need us. Our security is based totally on his love and not on our satisfying his need of us.

Christian leaders can harbor the arrogant notion that God needs them around. Some will say, "I will live as long as God needs me." Yet many great saints died young or during their

prime years of ministry. Service is no more a guar-
antee of long life than good works are an assurance of prosperity.

Another danger is that when we try to obligate
God by service, we can become very possessive of
our efforts and resent sharing the recognition with
others. We are anxious to receive the credit for
our service, as if God valued the work rather than
the motive. We become selfish in our service, not
wanting to share the work for fear God will not
recognize our sacrificial works of piety.

A great spiritual release came to me after five
years of strict Calvinist teaching on God's sovereignty. I came to the spiritual conviction that
God does not need me. He loves me. He gives me
the opportunity to perform for my maturity in
Christ. It is for *my* good, not *his* good.

—Fred Smith Sr.

103

REFLECTION

Do I spend some time regularly—in worship, in private devotions—simply extolling the majesty and awesome otherness of the Almighty? How might this be a corrective to the subtle trap of "domesticating" God?

PRAYER

Read Psalm 145.

"Aslan is not a tame lion."

—C. S. Lewis, *The Lion, the Witch, and the Wardrobe*

27

GOD'S WORK IN US

Your Words Came Out

*I can do everything with the help
of Christ who gives me the
strength I need.*
PHILIPPIANS 4:13

A S A NEW leader in ministry outside the local church, I was challenged, stretched, and often terrified. When a group of Pentecostal leaders from around the United States invited me to speak to them, I was both honored and nervous. To ease my jitters, I went in the night before I was due to speak, just to get to know the people and to worship with them. To understand the humor here, I come from a mainline Presbyterian background and had not yet been exposed to other styles of worship.

The music was wonderful. As the evening progressed, I was beginning to understand that this was a very different worship experience from any I had ever had. I was overwhelmed! I could not even focus on my own prayers because of the energy and the noise of this large group gathered in prayer. I fled to my room, and the first thing I did was to send my ministry team an e-mail asking for direction and prayer. I must admit, I also had a very frank and serious dialog with God about his putting me in this situation. I asked how a Presbyterian woman could have anything to say that would be heard in this very different culture. I reminded him that he had placed me there and I needed him—right now!

The next morning, after precious little sleep, as

I walked into the auditorium and was received by this loving group of people, I simply prayed, "God, be in my mouth." I have never experienced such a calm as I did walking up those stairs, for I had come to trust that God would never leave me alone in speaking his message.

What happened next was quite amazing. The interactive nature of the group, while new to me, was both affirming and supportive. The words flowed, and I delivered the message. The response was extraordinary and flattering—but also a little confusing. Weeks later I received an audiotape of my message. I listened in stunned silence. I could not believe I was the one speaking! God answered my prayers and indeed, through the Holy Spirit, his words were in my mouth.

—Sue Mallory

REFLECTION

When have I felt the undeniable presence of God in my life?

PRAYER

Dear God, thank you for showing up, for always being there. Help me to continue to grow in the confidence that you are always there, in good times and in bad, and that it is in you that I find my courage and strength.

"Act as though it were impossible to fail."

—Winston Churchill (1874–1965),
British statesman

108

28

GOD'S WORTHINESS

Feet on Earth, Head in Heaven

*In everything we do we try to
show that we are true ministers of
God. We patiently endure
troubles and hardships and
calamities of every kind. We have
been beaten, been put in jail,
faced angry mobs, worked to
exhaustion, endured sleepless
nights, and gone without food.
We have proved ourselves by our
purity, our understanding, our
patience, our kindness, our sincere
love, and the power of the Holy
Spirit.*

2 CORINTHIANS 6:4-6

HELEN Roseveare is a short, no-nonsense Irish doctor with steely blue eyes and a wry wit. When I met her in 1994, she was a spry seventy and reminded me of a favorite elderly aunt or grandmother. Just looking at her, one would not guess that she had spent the better part of her life serving Christ as a medical missionary in Zaire (now the Congo)—or that she had been beaten and raped repeatedly by rebels during the Simba Rebellion of the early 1960s. Despite her incredible suffering and subsequent emotional breakdown, she managed to come back to work and accomplish amazing things for Christ in the jungles of that land.

I was in Kenya interviewing her for a radio program. As she spoke of her horrible experience with the rebels, a thunderstorm passed overhead and rain pounded on the tin roof of the cottage. When she was finished, she said, "I'll have nightmares tonight from this."

I said, "I would never have asked you for an interview if I had known it would have this effect on you."

She dismissed my remark with a short wave of her hand: "No, no. The Lord told me that if I'm going to tell this story, I can't be like a phonograph record. I'll have to feel each time I tell it."

Then she said something incredible: "People would ask me, 'Was it worth all the suffering—what you accomplished there?' And I'd tell them, no, it's been too costly. All I got done doesn't offset what I paid personally.

"But then the Lord spoke to me. He said, 'Helen, that's the wrong question. The question is not, Was it worth it? The question is, Am I worthy?' And I said, 'Of course you are, Lord. You are worthy.'"

I was talking that day with a woman set right side up, her head in heaven and her feet planted firmly on the earth.

—Ben Patterson

REFLECTION

Do I believe that such devotion is really attainable by "ordinary" Christians? If so, what am I doing about it? If not, how can I open myself up to God's refining work?

PRAYER

Father, thank you for the example of godly leaders such as Helen Roseveare. Help me not merely to admire them from afar but to be inspired by them to follow your example.

"All the holy men seem to have gone off and died. There's no one left but us sinners to carry on the ministry."

—Jamie Buckingham, author

112

29

GRACE

Singled Out

*She thought he was the gardener.
"Sir," she said, "if you have taken
him away, tell me where you have
put him, and I will go and get
him."*

"Mary!" Jesus said.

*She turned toward him and
exclaimed, "Teacher!"*

JOHN 20:15-16

IN *Saving Private Ryan,* the compelling movie about World War II, a turning point comes when Captain Miller and his band of soldiers find Private Ryan. Since Ryan's three brothers have already died in action, the unit is charged with finding him and bringing him safely from the front so that he might be sent home. But Ryan says he doesn't want to return. His fellow soldiers, he argues, have suffered losses and need him.

Then one of Captain Miller's soldiers says to Ryan, "Two of us died buyin' you this ticket home." At that moment it is as if Ryan has been hit by a bullet.

Ryan asks, "What were their names?"

"Wade and Caparzo," the soldier answers.

Ryan repeats them quietly, then says to Captain Miller, "Sir, this doesn't make any sense. What have I done to deserve special treatment?"

If there is one clear turning point in the first Easter, one moment when the lights go on, it is that moment when Mary Magdalene hears her name from the lips of Jesus (John 20:16). Until that point there are only tears, bewilderment, and disappointment. After Mary hears her name, she understands; she sees the Lord and grasps the truth of his resurrection—and everything changes.

Jesus did not die for us as some nebulous throng of indistinguishable souls—he died for us as individuals with names, people created by God and precious to him. Jesus gave himself and searched us out, calling us by name.

With Private Ryan, we say, "This doesn't make any sense. What have I done to deserve special treatment?" But with Mary Magdalene, we say, "I have seen the Lord!"

—Harry Heintz

REFLECTION

When did I first realize that I was a name to God, a person whom he loved as an individual?

PRAYER

Oh, God, giver of every perfect gift, I don't know why you chose to grant me the greatest gift of all—your salvation in Christ. I know I haven't earned it! But let me, humbly and thankfully, live in such a way as to respond to that gift.

"Your life is not like a gift; your life is a gift. That is a very important grammatical point. And until you learn to receive your life gift, you are lost."

—Stanley Hauerwas, theologian and writer

GRACE

Can We Despise God's Grace?

*I gave you his house and his wives
and the kingdoms of Israel and
Judah. And if that had not been
enough, I would have given you
much, much more. Why, then,
have you despised the word of the
Lord and done this horrible deed?
For you have murdered Uriah
and stolen his wife. From this
time on, the sword will be a
constant threat to your family,
because you have despised me by
taking Uriah's wife to be your
own.*

2 SAMUEL 12:8-10

WHEN my two children were born, I assumed that each would be a star athlete someday. I pictured my son hitting home runs, throwing touchdown passes, dunking basketballs. My daughter would certainly be an Olympic-caliber gymnast, volleyball player, or soccer star. Yet both went on to have careers in music. I was, I have to admit, frustrated. Musicians were all well and good, I thought, but they weren't athletic heroes.

In my disappointment I was at risk of committing the sin the prophet Nathan warns David against in 2 Samuel 12: the sin of despising God's grace. God had given me two talented children who loved him and wanted to serve him, yet I was frustrated because they were not what *I* wanted them to be.

Thank God I did not miss his grace. I have come to love and deeply appreciate the talents my children have so graciously been given.

David, too, had been abundantly gifted by God, as the above text indicates: a kingship, an entire nation, and even the former king's harem. But it wasn't enough. David wanted more, and he pursued and slept with Bathsheba, another man's wife. In the process David committed murder, adultery, and, according to Nathan, the even more grievous sin of despising God's grace.

—Paul Borden

REFLECTION

Do I take seriously enough the idea that gratitude is more than a nice sentiment? How do I express my gratitude to God?

PRAYER

Father of Lights, all good gifts come from you. Grant me a grateful heart, and keep me from too much restless wanting.

"It is right to be contented with what we have, but never with what we are."

—Sir James Mackintosh (1765–1832)

HUMILITY

True Greatness

If I could speak in any language in heaven or on earth but didn't love others, I would only be making meaningless noise like a loud gong or a clanging cymbal.

1 CORINTHIANS 13:1

IN THE denomination in which I serve, many leaders volunteer on boards and oversee national ministry areas. I'm constantly challenged and thrilled by this sleek and sophisticated corporate world. One weekend I was invited to participate in one of the board's high-intensity meetings, and I was proud when I kept up with the complicated discussions. I was funny, perceptive, and well prepared—all leadership gifts God had blessed me with. The experience was very affirming.

But leaving that corporate boardroom for my rural parish was disheartening. Most of my parishioners, many of whom are retired, have never even lived outside the county. The fast pace and constant change of the business world is foreign to their experience. I felt that they didn't appreciate my abilities.

When I arrived home, I unenthusiastically visited a terminally ill man. His wife answered the door, obviously exhausted from a night of caring for him, and said, "Janet and Mel, our friends, are coming over to stay with Joe while I take a nap. Would you mind sitting with him until they arrive? They wanted to talk and pray with you."

When Mel came, he walked over to his lifelong friend and said, "Joe, it's Mel here. Give me your hand, and we'll just sit." Mel's palm held his friend's forehead in a tender blessing. "I love you, Joe," he said before kissing that same forehead. Still holding Joe's hand, Mel sat down with Janet and me. Intermittently Joe would moan, and Mel assured him of his presence and that he loved him.

We closed our time together with prayer. As I left, I glanced through the picture window to see Mel rearranging Joe's pillows, the whole time holding his friend's hand. That day I had seen true greatness—greatness you often don't experience in the boardroom. It humbled me.

—Mary C. Miller

123

REFLECTION

Do I unconsciously peg people as "important" or "not important" and treat them accordingly?

PRAYER

Lord Jesus, you loved the weak, the sick, the poor. I would follow your lead—but, if I'm honest, I admit that I, too, often prefer the strong, the healthy, the comfortable. Forgive my lack of compassion, and help me to see beyond the surface.

"True heroism is remarkably sober, very undramatic. It is not the urge to surpass all others at whatever cost, but the urge to serve others at whatever cost."

—Arthur Ashe, late tennis star

IDENTITY

Bringing Your Identity to Work

*I wait quietly before God, for my
salvation comes from him. He
alone is my rock and my
salvation, my fortress where I will
never be shaken.*

PSALM 62:1-2

IF YOU'RE a banker and you go to work one day and your bank has just merged and it doesn't need you anymore, your identity has just been taken away from you.

If your identity is being a husband, and your wife just fell in love with her tennis instructor and lets you know that she wants half and is out the door, your identity is gone.

The question of who we are is one of those profound questions that even successful people have not necessarily answered. In fact, our discovery of identity is complicated by our success. The more successful we are in our fields, the more most people tend to put us in a niche.

I had a serious auto accident, and when neurologists looked at me, they said, "You're going to be fine. We just don't know whether you're going to have your mental edge and your memory."

I said, "Can I tell you what I do for a living? I stand for an hour in front of people every weekend trying to convince them that I'm one step ahead of them on the most important issues of life, and I do it from memory!"

What I had to deal with was, "Do I *find* my identity at work or do I *bring* my identity to work?"

—Bob Shank

REFLECTION

What's the difference between finding my identity at work and bringing my identity to work?

PRAYER

Lord, you formed and shaped me while I was still in the womb. Help me to understand who you've created me to be and not substitute that with anything else.

"Self-knowledge grows out of a man's self-confrontation with God."

—Dietrich von Hildebrand (1889–1977)

33

INTEGRITY

Never Say Never

*If you think you are standing
strong, be careful, for you, too,
may fall into the same sin.*

1 CORINTHIANS 10:12

I FOUGHT back tears as my ten-year-old daughter leaned over and whispered in my ear, "Dad, you'll never do that to us, will you?" We were listening to a young woman in a Christian college choir share her story. The loving home environment in which she grew up was suddenly shattered when her dad unexpectedly walked out on the family. It was an all-too-familiar story: Another woman captured his heart, and so he abandoned his wife of almost twenty years.

In response to my daughter's question, I whispered back, "I promise that I won't." Later, as I reflected on this exchange, I realized that I had answered honestly. Making that promise was appropriate. But I could not, with integrity, say, "I will never do anything like that."

Some Christians—including some Christian leaders—see an admission of vulnerability as a sign of spiritual immaturity. The apostle Paul, however, considered it a sign of spiritual maturity. He confessed, "I discipline my body like an athlete, training it to do what it should. Otherwise, I fear that after preaching to others I myself might be disqualified" (1 Cor. 9:27). Then, as if anticipating a self-righteous response from his readers, he pointed them to the nation of Israel. No nation ever had the spiritual privileges Israel possessed—from the parting of the Red Sea to the presence of Christ (10:1-4). But they still blew it. They caved in to complaining, idolatry, and sexual immorality. Paul cites the people of Israel as "Exhibit A" of what can happen even to people who seem to be closest to God. Then he issues his classic warning against falling.

I don't know any Christian leaders who intended to pursue extramarital affairs. I don't know any Christian leaders who began their ministries with the aim of embezzling or misusing funds. I don't know any Christian leaders who planned on becoming bitter or walking away from their faith. But it happens. Just as eating a high-fat diet increases the risk of heart disease, assuming that "it will never happen to me" increases the risk of moral failure.

Leaders of integrity promise to walk in integrity. But they maintain their integrity by admitting vulnerability.

—Steve Mathewson

131

REFLECTION

In what areas of my character am I particularly "at risk"? How could I strengthen these areas against sin?

PRAYER

Father of Lights, my Rock and my Redeemer, you do not change. In you there are no shifting shadows. But I am weak and prone to wander. Hold me, Lord, and strengthen me. Let me abide always in your unfailing love.

"Whenever a man or a woman fails to walk with God, he or she walks on the edge of an abyss."

—Haddon Robinson, professor of preaching

34

INTEGRITY

Sir Paul Goes to the Palace

Now glory be to God! By his mighty power at work within us, he is able to accomplish infinitely more than we would ever dare to ask or hope. May he be given glory in the church and in Christ Jesus forever and ever through endless ages. Amen.

EPHESIANS 3:20-21

POP star Paul McCartney—now Sir Paul—spoke with reporters shortly after he was knighted in England. He had been thrilled to accept the invitation to Buckingham Palace. Older than most rock idols, McCartney had been raised to respect the royals, so to receive Britain's highest honor from the queen herself was the experience of a lifetime. During the ceremony he said to his wife, "Pinch me! Am I really here?" He was in a reverie, remembering his working-class boyhood in Liverpool, when, like any good musician, he became aware of the background music the orchestra was playing. "I'm gonna wash that man right out of my hair!" the brass blared. He laughed out loud, amused at the contrast between the brassy Broadway tune and the solemn ritual of the ancient ceremony.

Reflecting at the end of the interview, he said, "I guess the queen fancies show tunes. It's a good thing she does, or I would have lost it in the sheer glory of it all."

Sir Paul's observation is relevant to Christian leaders. Many believers are tempted to bifurcate life into the "secular" and "spiritual." It certainly would seem easier some days. How do we integrate our Sunday worship with our daily work? What does our weekly Bible study have to do with the movie we saw Friday night? How would our hairstylist or car mechanic fit in at church? What do we even know about their spiritual lives?

As I drive to church each Sunday morning, I tune in to a radio show called *Songs for the Christian Year.* But within five minutes my car stereo drifts into a band that carries the news, so for a while I have news and Christian music playing simultaneously and in equal volume. It's frustrating! At times I continue to sing loudly over the news; at other times I turn up the volume and listen very carefully to a breaking news story. I have to pay attention, deciding what message to listen to when.

135

In the same way, we who are saved by Christ are called to live fully in two worlds. It's a tension, balancing the show tune with the solemn ceremony, the high sacred moment with the messy ordinariness of the everyday. But as we seek to bring together these two worlds and balance the tension, God will abundantly accomplish his purposes.

—Mary C. Miller

REFLECTION

How integrated are the secular and the sacred in my life?

PRAYER

Jesus, help me to think of ways to bring the spiritual into my secular world in a way that brings honor and glory to you.

"It could be that one of the greatest hindrances to evangelism today is the poverty of our own experience."

—Billy Graham, evangelist

136

35

INTEGRITY

The "God Compartment"

He existed before everything else began, and he holds all creation together.

COLOSSIANS 1:17

O UR lives are complicated, and many demands divide our hearts. This is the essence of the integrity problem: We are people with divided hearts.

A large portion of our hearts is dedicated to being successful at work and in our relationships. Other parts are devoted to dreams for the future and hurts of the past. Still another part is devoted to Jesus Christ. We would love to give him more, but we must confront the fact that there are few compartments left over.

Each compartment has a different set of rules, and we conduct ourselves differently at different times depending on which part of the heart we are satisfying. This is why outwardly moral people do immoral things in private. This is also why we think we need to be aggressive in the workplace but loving and tender at home or at church. And this is why we live with secrets we hope will never come to light.

Moving from one compartment of life to another, we enter different worlds where we hold different identities, each wanting to grow and hold sway over our hearts. After a while our hearts tear apart because of the competition, and the walls that divide the compartments start to break down. It is at this point that people start to leave their families, churches, and the faith, saying, "I can't keep living a lie." The problem is, they're lying to themselves if they think they can heal their hearts on their own.

The message of the gospel is that a divided heart can be repaired, though not by ourselves. When we confront that truth, we discover the deeper truth of God's power that transforms every part of the heart, the power that breaks down those competing little worlds and unites our souls in the integrity of serving our Savior.

—M. Craig Barnes

139

REFLECTION

How would it change your life if you had to do everything in public? Even more sobering is the fact that everything we do is done in front of God.

PRAYER

Oh, God, in the course of my life I have carved up so much of my heart that there is precious little to give to you. So I ask that you will find all of the pieces I have given away and bind them together again with a deep love for Christ, my Savior.

"Integrity is keeping my commitment even if the circumstances when I made the commitment have changed."

—David Jeremiah, pastor, author, and speaker

140

36

JOY

Hints of Heaven

*When I look at the night sky and
see the work of your fingers—the
moon and the stars you have set in
place—what are mortals that you
should think of us, mere humans
that you should care for us?*

PSALM 8:3-4

WE HAD been hiking all day in the mountains of the Czech Republic, and around three o'clock, with our camp nowhere in sight, we all felt tired and cranky. There were about fifteen of us—leaders and high school students from a summer evangelistic camp. The sun burned brightly in the afternoon light, and the sweat dried on our faces and necks, leaving a crusty feeling. We had reached the stage of the hike I dreaded—feeling overcome by a numbing weariness and lacking strength just to put one heavy foot in front of the other.

For fifteen minutes straight I thought only about the blister on my heel and about the fact that my water had run out an hour before. I stopped enjoying the breathtaking scenery of the mountains and fixated on my feet. With my pace slowing, I knew the end would be longer in coming. I started to encourage myself, thinking, *It isn't so bad; nobody has ever died from sore feet.*

As we descended the mountain, the path opened up into a clearing in the trees, and the hillside sloped gently into a small riverbed. We could see our campsite below us, and the tall grass was filled with short, scraggly bushes. Upon closer inspection we discovered, to our great delight, that the bushes were full of ripe blueberries.

Without discussion we each found our place in the grass and began to eat.

Almost imperceptibly the collective mood began to change. We laughed and insisted on showing each other every perfect, purple, plump berry we discovered. As we chatted, we flashed purple smiles, and our faces, fingers, and shirts bore the marks of our indulgence. Our troop dotted the hillside—stooping down or sitting in the middle of the berry patch as we delightfully picked, examined, and then popped berries into our mouths. Soon I lay on my back, blissfully satiated and soaking in the warmth of the afternoon sun.

143

That is what I imagine heaven to be like. Not only were my hunger and thirst satisfied, but I felt I had tasted something more than fresh blueberries—an intimation of the life to come. In the contentment of my rest stop on the mountainside, I considered heaven as the full satisfaction of our longing. God is preparing for his children a place where happiness is deep and lasting.

—Linda Gehrs

REFLECTION

What glimpses of heaven has God recently sent my way?

PRAYER

Creator God, thank you for those occasional mountaintop reminders that life is about more than the daily routine. When the routine gets tedious and I wonder where you are, help me to remember those times when you've declared, "Look! Here I am!"

"If worship is just one thing we do, everything becomes mundane. If worship is the one thing we do, everything takes on eternal significance."

—Timothy J. Christenson

37

JOY

The Roots of a Joyful Spirit

*I have told you this so that you
will be filled with my joy. Yes,
your joy will overflow!*
JOHN 15:11

IN A YARD two blocks from my house the trees are dying. For some time my wife and I, on our neighborhood walks, have noticed something wrong—fewer leaves on branches, peeling bark, a greenish white discoloration here and there. Two years ago it began with a large maple. Then the sickness spread to two evergreens.

Last night as we walked by, we saw just a few leaves scattered over the entire maple. My wife said, "I'm sure glad we don't live next door." Indeed, I felt like walking on the other side of the street.

A leader who regularly lacks joy can resemble those dying trees. Paul wrote, "Worldly sorrow brings death" (2 Cor. 7:10, NIV). God does not want anyone to live a grim Christian life or lead a grinding, heavyhearted ministry. Such leadership reflects a spiritual disease that can be contagious to followers, and it happens even in numerically successful ministries.

In this area of joy, leaders face two unique temptations.

First, we are tempted to link our joy to the progress we are making toward our goals and vision. We long to see God's work move forward, and we rightly grieve over setbacks. Spiritual illness sets in, though, when we rejoice more in success than we do in the Lord or when we cannot rejoice in the Lord in the midst of ministry trials. Paul said of himself that he was "sorrowful, yet always rejoicing" (2 Cor. 6:10, NIV).

Second, sometimes we consciously or unconsciously want to signal our followers that something is wrong, like parents who occasionally must frown at a teenager's study habits. If a wide gap stands between where our people are and where God wants them to be, at times leaders need to communicate that everything is not sweetness and light. But spiritual sickness sets in when a leader's frown is unremitting, when a smile does not return after there is repentance. Then a leader's hard look becomes destructively manipulative.

Jesus was a joyful leader who brought not only a serious mission but also his divine joy! Of the fruit of the Spirit listed in Galatians 5:22-23, joy holds the second position on the list—just after love.

Like a tall tree that is lush with green leaves and seeds, there is vibrant spiritual health in a leader and a ministry that overflows with joy.

—Craig Brian Larson

147

REFLECTION

Am I predominantly joyful or sorrowful? If the latter, what are the root causes?

PRAYER

Oh, God, keep me from being a heavyhearted leader. When trials and difficulties threaten to rob me of joy or overwhelm me with anger and frustration, keep my eyes focused on you and my faith firmly rooted in your truth.

"Anger is a joy killer. We simply cannot be grateful and angry, or joyful and angry. While joy is a gift, it is also something I need to choose."

—Ben Patterson, pastor and writer

38

LORDSHIP OF CHRIST

The Difference between Profit and Prosperity

He will give you all you need from day to day if you live for him and make the Kingdom of God your primary concern.

MATTHEW 6:33

D URING the second year of my career in investment banking, several of my colleagues and I left the company where we worked and assembled a new firm to compete in a niche of municipal finance that had not yet fully matured. In those early years we often remarked that our philosophy of management could be summarized as "revenues exceeding expenses." We soon discovered that being prosperous meant more than simply being profitable.

Every business enterprise must ultimately be profitable to accomplish its purposes. Yet simply earning a profit is an incomplete organizational objective. As owners we needed to concern ourselves with additional issues, such as employee benefits, staff development, and strategic planning. As time passed, we became better managers, and our firm experienced impressive growth in both earnings and market presence. Had we focused only on profitability and not taken a holistic approach to our business, I am convinced our results would have been measurably different.

In my desire to follow the teachings of Jesus Christ, there are times I have been satisfied with only the most *profitable* matter of my faith—eternal life. Yet I have learned that when I center my thinking only on salvation, I miss out on the broader blessings of the Christian experience. Jesus said that we should seek the fullness of faith in him and follow his example of righteous living. Our spiritual journey should not end when we offer our lives to Jesus and seek his forgiveness for our sins. Rather, he should have ownership over every department of our lives. We should not be satisfied with anything less than to have Jesus reign supreme in every relationship and in every responsibility.

I will admit this is a challenging assignment. We naturally try to control our lives rather than yield them to Jesus. We tend to rely on our impulses rather than turn our hearts to heaven. But when I am in fellowship with others who follow Jesus, and when I seek to serve rather than to be served, I undergo spiritual growth and sense the presence of God in my life. When I go beyond a spiritual "profit motive" and pursue a relationship with Christ to its depth and breadth, I know true prosperity—the only prosperity that endures.

—Dave Sveen

REFLECTION

Are there areas of my life I'm unwilling to open up to the gaze of Christ?

PRAYER

Lord, create in me a spirit of surrender. Help me resist the urge to grab control of my own life. Open my hands and heart to you.

"One does not surrender a life in an instant. That which is lifelong can only be surrendered in a lifetime."

—Jim Elliot, twentieth-century missionary martyr

152

39

LOVE FOR GOD

One Surpassing Love

If you love your father or mother more than you love me, you are not worthy of being mine; or if you love your son or daughter more than me, you are not worthy of being mine. If you refuse to take up your cross and follow me, you are not worthy of being mine. If you cling to your life, you will lose it; but if you give it up for me, you will find it.

MATTHEW 10:37-39

Perpetua was a Christian noblewoman who, at the turn of the third century A.D., lived with her husband, her son, and her slave, Felicitas, in Carthage (modern-day Tunis). At this time North Africa was the center of a vibrant Christian community, so when Emperor Septimius Severus determined to cripple Christianity, he focused his attention there.

Among the first to be arrested were five new Christians taking classes to prepare for baptism, one of whom was Perpetua.

Her father, a pagan, immediately came to her in prison. He saw an easy way for Perpetua to save herself: He entreated her simply to deny she was a Christian.

"Father, do you see this vase here?" she replied. "Could it be called by any other name than what it is?"

"No," he replied.

"Well, neither can I be called anything other than what I am, a Christian."

A few days later he returned and pleaded, "Have pity on my gray head. . . . Give up your pride!"

Perpetua was deeply touched but remained unshaken.

On the day of the hearing Perpetua and her

friends were marched before the governor, Hilarianus. Perpetua's friends were questioned first, each in turn admitting to being a Christian and each in turn refusing to make a sacrifice (in an act of emperor worship). Then the governor turned to question Perpetua.

At that moment Perpetua's father, carrying her son in his arms, burst into the room. He grabbed Perpetua and pleaded, "Perform the sacrifice. Have pity on your baby!"

Hilarianus, probably wishing to avoid the unpleasantness of executing a mother who still suckled a child, added, "Have pity on your father's gray head; have pity on your infant son. Offer the sacrifice for the welfare of the emperors."

155

Perpetua replied simply: "I will not."

"Are you a Christian then?" asked the governor.

"Yes, I am," Perpetua replied.

Her father interrupted again, but Hilarianus had heard enough: He condemned Perpetua and her friends to die in the arena.

Like many martyr stories, part of this may be exaggerated. But what stands out to even the cautious reader is a clear picture of a young mother whose love for God made all other loves pale by comparison.

—Mark Galli

REFLECTION

What "loves" threaten to surpass my love for God?

PRAYER

Lord, help me to order my life and my devotion so that I love family and friends as you've called me to love them, and to love you ever more deeply still.

"He who offers to God a second place offers him no place."

—John Ruskin, English author and philanthropist (1819–1900)

40

MATERIALISM

A Tale of Two Tables

*Better is a dinner of vegetables
where love is than a fatted ox and
hatred with it.*

PROVERBS 15:17, NRSV

A T ONE table there is bounty, elegance, roast beef, rich sauce, fine wine. The table bespeaks achievement, status, all that the world has to offer—in Solomon's time and in ours. At the other table the diners divide up a meager portion of greens and bread, without costly seasonings, served in rough bowls. Who wouldn't want to be the dinner guest at the first table?

Yet here and elsewhere the ancient teacher of proverbial wisdom warns against the seductions of the good life and points to right priorities with the repeated phrase, "Better a _____ than a _____." "Better a little with the fear of the Lord than great wealth with turmoil" (15:16, NIV). "Better a little with righteousness than much gain with injustice" (16:8, NIV). "Better a dry crust with peace and quiet than a house full of feasting, with strife" (17:1, NIV).

The message is clear: Wealth really isn't very important. Neither is impressing the neighbors or showing off one's achievements. Living a godly life is important. Healthy, God-honoring relationships are important.

It's a lesson we've heard before, but Proverbs really piles it on, one after the other, and the vividness and succinctness characteristic of Solomon add impact to the reminder.

It's a lesson we in Christian leadership do well to heed. Not because many of us are in danger of making too much money—if anything, many of us have knowingly surrendered economic gain for the sake of serving God's people. Yet preoccupation with striving, getting, and accumulating is not limited to unbelievers or those with six-figure incomes.

In the last several years our culture has raised the bar on what an "adequate lifestyle" looks like. Particularly if you live in a middle-class, white-collar community, you're aware of this phenomenon. The new houses being built are minipalaces, and parked in the driveways of those minipalaces are minivans or sport-utility vehicles. Many teenagers think nothing of plunking down fifty dollars of their money—or yours—for an Abercrombie & Fitch sweater. And that computer that seemed so cutting-edge five years ago is now a worthless relic.

Christian leaders are, for the most part, no longer forced to live in near poverty. Our lifestyles in many ways aren't all that different from our neighbors' across the street. But precisely because of this, we need to take great care that our priorities remain in line with God's Word, that worldly desires don't sneak up on us.

159

I recall Richard Neuhaus telling us young pastors, "There is no more important decision that you can make as a young minister than to decide how much money you and your family will need to be happy. A pastor can sell his soul for a mere two-hundred-fifty-dollar-a-year raise."

I think he's right: It's important to make a decision. Which table would you like to be invited to? How much are you willing to pay to be able to sit there?

—William Willimon

REFLECTION

If someone told me to divest myself of my posses-
sions, which would be hardest to give up, and why?

PRAYER

God, I submit myself to your pruning. Guard my
heart against covetousness; help me to hold posses-
sions lightly, and keep my mind in line with that of
your Son, who never owned much of anything and
yet was and is everything.

*"Almost all reformers, however strict their social con-
science, live in houses as big as they can pay for."*

—Logan Pearsall Smith, author

PEACE

Greater Than Our Accomplishments

"Be silent, and know that I am God! I will be honored by every nation. I will be honored throughout the world." The Lord Almighty is here among us; the God of Israel is our fortress.

PSALM 46:10-11

MOST of us view success as fame, accomplishment, and acquisition. Our society has chosen personality over character. But Christian success must be built of character, not of personality or skill. The great qualities in life are involved in the character of people—their wisdom, integrity, honesty, loyalty, faith, forgiveness, and love.

The *New Century Version* of the Bible gives an interesting translation of Psalm 131:1-2: "Lord, my heart is not proud; I don't look down on others. I don't do great things, and I can't do miracles. But I am calm and quiet."

How can we claim Christian success unless our hearts are calm and quiet? Thomas Kelly, the eminent Quaker philosopher, said that inside each person there should be a quiet center that nothing can disturb. The great Christian mystics continually talked of the throne of God, which is in the innermost part of our heart, where no storm, tribulation, or temptation can disturb.

Scripture says, "It is better to have self-control than to conquer a city" (Prov. 16:32). Obviously our condition is more than our accomplishment. In other words, our greatest accomplishment is our condition.

—Fred Smith Sr.

REFLECTION

What one thing could I let go of this week and trust God to take care of?

PRAYER

Father, I do not feel calm and quiet; the noise in my head seems to be growing louder. I give to you the issue that dominates my thinking.

"It is man's business to do the will of God; God takes on Himself the special care of that man; therefore that man ought never to be afraid of anything."

—George Macdonald, nineteenth-century pastor and writer

42

PERSEVERANCE

The God Who Perseveres

Dear brothers and sisters,
whenever trouble comes your way,
let it be an opportunity for joy.
For when your faith is tested, your
endurance has a chance to grow.

JAMES 1:2-3

I HAVE never won a race and probably never will. My stride is unpolished and could use a good measure of fine-tuning. Running doesn't come naturally—it's very difficult for me. My knees are often tender, my feet ache, and my back is almost always sore.

So why do I run? I run because running gives me energy; it burns those extra pounds that tend to accumulate as I age, and at night I easily fall fast asleep.

Because running is not a natural activity for me, I have to motivate myself to lace up my Nikes and head out the door. Without fail, at the end of my daily run I feel good about myself. I have faced the dragon and lived to run another day!

Often we view our Christian faith in a similar light. As we encounter the usual challenges of this race called life, our approach is often to reach deep into our souls for strength and then hope we can keep plodding away to a righteous finish. But when James encouraged the first-century church to persevere, I'm not sure this is what he had in mind. As I have thought through the Bible's instruction on perseverance, I have concluded that perseverance has more to do with our knowing who God is and less to do with our own efforts toward successfully overcoming life's challenges.

Perseverance is a quality of God's character. God perseveres with us in our struggles, and he never gives up on us. His desire is that we will turn to him for strength and courage rather than look to ourselves, to other people, or to things for help. Victory in overcoming trials is muted if it occurs apart from God's perseverance in our lives. The Bible teaches us that our faith will grow and become mature if we turn to God as trouble invades our turf.

As certain as the sun rises in the east, we will confront challenges that seem insurmountable. Fortunately, we don't need to turn inward for the strength to persevere. Rather, God stands ready to hold us in his hands if we turn to him for help. Just as I gain physical strength from my daily run, we gain spiritual strength from God's persevering presence in our lives. It should not be surprising that James considered the trials of life as opportunities for spiritual growth!

—Dave Sveen

REFLECTION

When I'm struggling or discouraged or feeling over-whelmed, what is my typical response? Where and to whom do I turn?

PRAYER

Lord, I don't know if I can honestly say, like James, that I see troubles as "an opportunity for joy." But when they come, help me to always seek first your face, your hand, and your leading through the storm; help me to ask, "Father, what are you trying to teach me through this?"

"God's Word often refers to the Christian experience as a walk, seldom as a run, and never as a mad dash."

—Steven J. Cole

168

⌖ PERSEVERANCE

The Warehouse with Wings

O God, have mercy on me. The enemy troops press in on me. My foes attack me all day long. My slanderers hound me constantly, and many are boldly attacking me.

PSALM 56:1-2

A T ONE ministry conference I stood during a break, visiting with a pastor friend. He described some of the good things happening at his church and then cautioned, "That doesn't mean we don't have our share of frustrations."

"I don't know any pastor who isn't frustrated," I responded.

For leaders of any sort of ministry, frustration is the nature of the work.

In fact, the better you are as a leader, the more frustration you may be in for. Leaders have grand vision, and great visions aren't reached overnight. Leaders want the best for everyone, and not everyone reaches their best. Leaders are goal oriented, and in the path of every worthwhile kingdom goal stand many setbacks and obstacles. Leaders are people oriented, and where there are people, there are problems. Leaders demand a lot of themselves, yet they all have human failings. Leaders are future oriented, yet they must live in the present. Leaders call for change, and most change meets with resistance.

So leadership by nature pushes against a high drag coefficient. Drag is the resistance air gives to the body of airplanes and automobiles as they move through air. Depending on the shape of an airplane wing, that drag is increased or decreased. As we strain to speed forward, sometimes it feels as though the leadership airplane is shaped like a warehouse with wings. The resistance is incredible. The drag on leadership is so great that it threatens to bring leaders to a grinding halt unless they have an extraordinary level of God-inspired perseverance.

Leadership is more about perseverance than about speed. Psalm 132:1 says, "Lord, remember David and all that he suffered." David was one of the greatest—and most successful—leaders in Israel's history, yet his life was marked by continual, extreme hardship.

For example, after the prophet Samuel anointed David as the next king of Israel, King Saul repeatedly attempted to kill David. David had to wander in the desert and in foreign lands for years as a fugitive with several hundred outcasts. Once, when David and his men were away from their town on a mission, an enemy burned their town and took all their wives and children. Not only did David face the loss of his own family, but his men talked of stoning him to death! David was the anointed leader of Israel, but he endured a lifetime of hardships as Israel's shepherd.

So don't be surprised by the drag coefficient of leadership. With God's help, you can endure it and overcome.

—Craig Brian Larson

171

REFLECTION

Am I willing to pay the price of perseverance to obey God's call to leadership? What are my expectations for the comfort level of leadership?

PRAYER

Lord, when the drag threatens to slow me down and weaken my resolve, help me to look to you for the strength and perseverance to endure the hardships that come with being a leader.

"Let me tell you the secret that has led me to my goal. My strength lies solely in my tenacity."

—Louis Pasteur, nineteenth-century scientist

44

PERSISTENCE

Can We Change God's Mind?

*Right away a woman came to
him whose little girl was possessed
by an evil spirit. She had heard
about Jesus, and now she came
and fell at his feet.*

MARK 7:25

WE CAN sometimes underestimate our responsibility before God—the things he wants us to do for ourselves.

Theologian P. T. Forsyth called God an "infinite opportunist." In prayer God invites us to enter into partnership with him in the working out of his immutable will in our lives and in the lives of others, giving us what Pascal called the "dignity of causality." In the mystery of the interaction between divine sovereignty and human freedom, there are some things God won't do until we ask.

The mystery goes deeper. Forsyth says that not only may persistent prayer change what God will do, but it may, in a sense, take the form of actually resisting what his will is in a particular instance. To resist his will can actually be to do his will. What this means is that in prayer we may sometimes resist what God desires to be only temporary and intermediary—and therefore to be transcended.

For example, I was born into a poor and relatively uneducated family. No one on either side of my family had gone to college. There were no books in my home when I was a child. That, I believe, was God's will for me. But was it also his will that I passively accept that as my fate, my foreordained situation in life? Or was it his will that I resist that circumstance and find a way to go to college, to find books and delight in them? I think it was. In other words, I was to resist his lower initial will in favor of his higher, more ultimate will.

At any given moment in our lives it may be

God's will that we face great pain and disappointment and loss. But God may also desire that we
resist his will in that moment in favor of his higher
and greater will. Sometimes we may beg and beg
and hear him refuse, as he did with Paul, and say,
"My grace is enough. It's all you need" (2 Cor.
12:9, paraphrase). But other times we may come
away, as did the blind man Bartimaeus, who would
not take no for an answer and finally got a yes from
Jesus (see Mark 10:46-52). It may be for us as it
was with a Gentile woman from Syrophoenicia.

She came to seek her daughter's deliverance
from a demon. What she initially got from Jesus
was a stiff retort. Using a figure that Jews com-
monly used of Gentiles, an insult, he called both
her and her people dogs: "First let the children eat
all they want . . . for it is not right to take the
children's bread and toss it to their dogs."

That may have turned me away, but not her. She
jumped right into the fray and jabbed back, saying,
"Yes, Lord, . . . but even the dogs under the table eat
the children's crumbs." Jesus loved it. He answered,
"For such a reply, you may go; the demon has left
your daughter" (Mark 7:24-30, NIV).

We may obey God as much when we push our
case and plead our cause as we do when we accept
his decision and say, "Yet not what I will, but
what you will."

—Ben Patterson

REFLECTION

How often do I really engage with God in prayer? Is prayer for me an ongoing and absolutely necessary conversation?

PRAYER

Lord, keep me speaking to you; keep me listening to you; and most important, keep me open to doing your will.

"I used to ask God to help me. Then I asked if I might help him. I ended up asking him to do his work through me."

—Hudson Taylor, nineteenth-century missionary to China

45

PRIDE

What You Don't See Can Hurt You

*Those who exalt themselves will
be humbled, and those who
humble themselves will be exalted.*
MATTHEW 23:12

IN *Let Your Life Speak* (Jossey-Bass, 1999)
Parker J. Palmer writes of five "shadows" in
leaders' lives. These deep, unconscious beliefs
cause harm to the leader and harm to other people. I retitle the shadows this way:

1. I am what I do.
2. This is a war—I must fight and win.
3. It all depends on me.
4. If we manage everything perfectly, we won't
   have to deal with chaos and pain.
5. Nothing can fail or die on my watch.

Pause for a moment. Before you read on, ask
yourself, and answer honestly, "Which of these
shadows, if any, have I lived and believed?"

A few months ago I asked myself that question.
I soon saw that at work, without realizing it, I
often act as if shadow number 3 were true: "It all
depends on me." This comically irrational but
somehow compelling belief causes me to give
unsolicited advice to others. As I confessed to a
friend over lunch, "I have enough energy and
opinions for my job and for everyone else's." I
sometimes feel like the guy who had a near-death
experience—and somebody else's life passed
before his eyes.

Obviously this is not helpful to others (who needs my unasked-for advice?) and is not healthy for me (I feel stress worrying about work that isn't even mine). So I'm trying to put off this lie so I can put on the truth: It does not all depend on me. I'm trying to slow down, catch my breath, listen more than I talk.

As I look at the list of leadership shadows, I think they all come from fear and, deeper still, from what the Bible would describe with a single word: *pride*. And the only way to deal with pride is to humble yourself before God.

Are you living and leading as if a shadow were substance? Then join me in praying the words of Thomas Merton: "Give me humility in which alone is rest, and deliver me from pride which is the heaviest of burdens."

—Kevin A. Miller

REFLECTION

Have I bought into one or more of the leadership shadows above? If so, in what ways could I put off the lie and put on the truth?

PRAYER

Lord, open my eyes to the lies I may have believed, lies that hinder my growth in effective leadership. Help me to put off pride and put on humility.

"Pride is at the bottom of all great mistakes."

—John Ruskin, English author and philanthropist
(1819–1900)

46

PURPOSE

What's in the Box?

He existed before everything else began, and he holds all creation together.

Christ is the head of the church, which is his body. He is the first of all who will rise from the dead, so he is first in everything.

COLOSSIANS 1:17-18

I WAS in my thirties, and I had already fulfilled my teenage dream: I was president and chairman of my own cable company; I was happily married and had a son who was exactly what every father hopes for; I was active in my church; and I was growing intellectually and culturally. I sincerely thought I had made it.

But like a thief in the night, the quiet intruder began disturbing my peace of mind. I began questioning where my success was leading me. I had perfected "the art of the deal" and took great pleasure in acquiring new assets. But what was I passing in the process?

The increasing turmoil over the direction of my life brought me to a strategic business consultant. Ignoring all my spreadsheets, lists of future projects, and notes about my strengths and weaknesses, this high-priced consultant asked me one simple question: "What's in the box?" He asked me to draw a square in the middle of my legal pad. Then he gave me an assignment.

He said, "I've been listening to you for two hours, and I can't help you unless you put one thing in the box. For you, it is either money or Jesus Christ." He then instructed me to draw a symbol inside the box that represented my life's central passion.

As I was deciding what to put in the box, I thought, *What if God asked me to sell my business and give all my money away?* Most of the time I felt God was a pretty good deal—if he didn't get in the way. But it was precisely my keeping him at arm's length that was causing the turmoil in my life. I had plenty of success, but what I really needed was significance.

Taking a deep breath, I reached for my pen and drew a little cross in the middle of the box. By doing that I was saying to God, "You are my primary loyalty. I am involved in many relationships, but no relationship will be as important to me from now on as you. If I have to choose, you're it."

I admit that drawing the little cross in the box was scary. Most of us really cling to our lives of property and privilege. We want to be in control. To "let go and let God" is fraught with risk and adventure. Today I still enjoy the thrill of doing deals, but instead of buying cable television systems, I am helping other successful people turn their faith into action.

183

If you are feeling discontented, I promise you that the still, small voice of God is inviting you to an enormous adventure that will be more fulfilling than any worldly success. I cannot tell you where it will lead. I can only tell you that the first step of this journey begins with making your life available to God. When you put him in the center of your life's box, you will begin to make the transition from success to significance.

—Bob Buford

REFLECTION

What is in the center of your box?

PRAYER

Lord Jesus, more than success or health or even happy relationships, I desire you. And I know that when I put you first, completely and without reservation, all of these other things will fall into place.

"God has no more precious gift to a church or an age than a man who lives as an embodiment of his will, and inspires those around him with the faith of what grace can do."

—Andrew Murray, nineteenth-century devotional writer and pastor

184

47

SELF-ACCEPTANCE

"I Am What I Am"

*Last of all, I saw him, too, long
after the others, as though I had
been born at the wrong time. For
I am the least of all the apostles,
and I am not worthy to be called
an apostle after the way I
persecuted the church of God.*

*But whatever I am now, it is
all because God poured out his
special favor on me.*

1 CORINTHIANS 15:8-10

FOR years I struggled with a low self-image. Mother married my father against the will of her parents. My father was an itinerant worker. He rode railroad freight cars to the Midwest, where he worked as a harvest laborer. Then he would return to his home in St. Paul and live on his wages. He was a kind person, soft-spoken, gentle, a good dancer, and very handsome, but my mother soon discovered that he was completely irresponsible. He never did support the family. My mother's father set him up in business twice, but my father never made it go.

When I was ten years old, my parents divorced—in a little North Dakota town where nobody got divorced—and we moved into a flat where we shared a bathroom with twenty families. I can still hear the cockroaches crush in the door jamb when I closed the door.

I've been afraid of my father's traits all of my life. To this day I feel there is something in me that wants to run as far away from responsibility as I can get.

After I became a Christian, a pastor helped me see my arrogance, that there was no substance to it and that I was covering up all those awful fears I had about myself and my inadequacy. He showed me how to study the Scriptures. The verse that helped me turn the corner was Paul's marvelous testimony that in weakness he became strong. I grabbed that truth with both hands as my valid place of self-acceptance; by the grace of God, I am what I am.

—Richard C. Halverson

REFLECTION

Do I see myself as God sees me—as a beloved child?

PRAYER

God of grace, thank you for reaching out to me even though I am inadequate, and thank you for embracing me in love.

"What a man thinks of himself, that it is which determines or rather indicates his fate."

—Henry David Thoreau (1817–1862),
American writer

48

SELF-INVENTORY

Habit Tracking

*Search me, O God, and know my
heart; test me and know my
thoughts. Point out anything in
me that offends you, and lead me
along the path of everlasting life.*

PSALM 139:23-24

HISTORIANS continue to puzzle over one of the great mysteries of history: how to explain the sixteenth century. In 1560 two movements dominated Europe, neither of which had existed twenty-five years earlier. The north was dominated by Calvinism, the south by the Jesuit order.

In 1534 Ignatius Loyola gathered the nucleus of his new order and took the vows of poverty, chastity, and obedience. In 1536 John Calvin arrived in Geneva. Twenty-five years later Europe had been changed. Nothing in the history of the world, not even the rise of Islam, can compare with the rapid growth and effectiveness of these institutions.

How do you explain it? Both were, by 1560, large institutions, each involving thousands of ordinary people, most of them working alone. Many worked under great pressure and danger, yet there were practically no defections and very few bad apples. What was the secret?

Today we understand it. Both Calvin and
Loyola taught a similar spiritual discipline: Whenever one does anything in a key activity (they were
usually spiritual activities but not entirely), one
writes it down, and then one keeps track of what
happens. This feedback, whether it's a Calvinist
examination of conscience or a Jesuit spiritual
exercise, is the way you quickly find out what
you're good at. And you also find out what your
bad habits are that inhibit full yield.

—Peter Drucker

191

REFLECTION

What key habits do I need in order to be more spiritually effective?

PRAYER

Help me to do an honest but gracious self-examination, Lord, not so as to condemn myself but to note areas where I need growth.

"It is when we face ourselves and face Christ, that we are lost in wonder, love, and praise. We need to rediscover the almost lost discipline of self-examination; and then a reawakened sense of sin will beget a reawakened sense of wonder."

—Andrew Murray, nineteenth-century author on the spiritual life

192

49

SPIRITUAL MATURITY

The Best Is Yet to Come

*"I know the plans I have for you,"
says the Lord. "They are plans for
good and not for disaster, to give
you a future and a hope."*

JEREMIAH 29:11

I NO longer believe that there is such a thing as a "simple surgery." A while back I went in for a so-called same-day procedure to have my gallbladder removed. I was supposed to be home by midafternoon, but there were some complications— actually, there were a lot of complications. I ended up with a twice-pierced aorta and lay in a coma for two weeks in the trauma ward of a large regional hospital. My blood pressure went down, and my body suffered a condition known as hypoxia. Because of lack of blood pressure to my lower spine, my legs don't function normally. I can walk, but I do so with a noticeable limp and at a slow pace. Stairs are difficult to negotiate.

Ironically, all this happened to someone who presurgery was a driven, type A personality. Much of that has changed now. One of my friends who knew me before the operation has dubbed me a "rabbit trapped in a turtle body."

While in the intensive care unit I was unable to talk (who can, with a respirator hose jammed down the throat?). But I did quite a bit of listening—to God. One thing I distinctly sensed the Lord showing me was his intention to "reimprint" me.

I remembered from an Introduction to Psychology class in college that baby ducks will identify as their mother the first moving object they

see upon coming out of their shell. As disciples of
Christ we are initially imprinted by the Spirit and
begin to walk a path of discipleship as arranged by
God. I believe now that God calls us as leaders to
be open to his reimprinting us from time to
time—to following a new path, a new normality
he has set for us. And because we know the character of God—that he is good and he is for
us—we know that the best is always yet to be for
us, regardless of our circumstances.

—Steve Sjogren

195

REFLECTION

Where in my life right now could I grow by being reimprinted by the power of the Holy Spirit?

PRAYER

Spirit of God, so work within me that I may truly grow and even rejoice in my current circumstances.

"I became my own only when I gave myself to Another."

—C. S. Lewis (1898–1963),
English novelist and essayist

50

SPIRITUAL WARFARE

Satan's a Bear

Humble yourselves, therefore, under God's mighty hand, that he may lift you up in due time. Cast all your anxiety on him because he cares for you.

Be self-controlled and alert. Your enemy the devil prowls around like a roaring lion looking for someone to devour. Resist him, standing firm in the faith, because you know that your brothers throughout the world are undergoing the same kind of sufferings.

1 PETER 5:6-9, NIV

IMAGINE hiking in Glacier National Park and finding a blue hat on the trail. Then you spot a camera on a tripod and a small red backpack. You ease back about thirty feet, senses on full alert. Your heart starts pounding when you find a pool of blood. It starts hammering when you see grizzly tracks, claw marks scratched into the hard-packed ground.

That's what Buck Wilde saw on a pleasant October Saturday in 1992. Buck followed the tracks, making plenty of noise. He found coins, a bootlace, a wristwatch, and finally, a man lying on his side. The man's body was warm, but Buck couldn't detect a pulse. He ran back to the red pack to grab a coat to cover the man. When he returned five minutes later, however, the man was gone. The bear had come back and moved the injured man. Buck never saw the grizzly, but he knew it was there.

That's how Satan operates. You can't see him, but he's lurking, poised to destroy. One of the weapons in his arsenal is suffering. First Peter is a letter that encourages believers to keep trusting God in times of trial and persecution. Peter points to such instigators of suffering as malicious gossips, cruel masters, and those who are disobedient. But in the last paragraph of the epistle, he finally identifies who's really behind suffering: Satan.

How do we counter his attacks? When trials come, our response often is to accuse God: "Lord, how could you let this happen to my child?" "Why don't you help me find a job?" "Why don't you do something about this church conflict?" Questions of God's involvement in our suffering (Does he cause it? use it to help us grow?) have been debated ever since Job. But one thing that is clear from Scripture is God's *care* for us in our suffering. In Peter's words, we are to "cast" our cares upon God.

Interestingly, there's only one other place in the New Testament where the original Greek word translated "cast" is found. It's in the story of Jesus' triumphal entry into Jerusalem. Following Jesus' instructions, his disciples bought a colt, and according to Luke 19:35 they "cast" or "threw" their cloaks upon it. Casting our problems on God, then, resembles tossing a blanket or a saddle on the back of a horse. We give God the burden.

In a fallen world, sorrow will come. Adversity will strike. But we don't have to give the enemy the advantage. We can affirm God's care for us, continually bringing our hurts and discouragements to him, opening ourselves to his healing compassion.

—Steve Mathewson

REFLECTION

How has Satan tried to use a difficult situation to discourage or frustrate me?

PRAYER

Lord, help me to remember that your might directs me, your power protects me, and your love envelopes me—in all circumstances.

"You cannot control the origin of your suffering, but you can control the outcome."

—Warren Wiersbe, pastor and author

200

51

STRESS

An Unseen Enemy

We were under great pressure, far
beyond our ability to endure.
2 Corinthians 1:8, NIV

I COULD have attributed the problems to unreliable or immature people, but I sensed something far deeper going on. We were engaged in spiritual warfare, struggling not against flesh and blood but against spiritual forces of evil in the heavenly realms (Eph. 6:12).

I shudder now to think of all that occurred: a highly respected staff member charged with sexual impropriety; wives of two elders, related by marriage, feuding over family issues; the Christian education department leaderless in the shift to summer schedule; a deacon in jail after his wife called 9-1-1; his wife in jail herself four nights later for driving while intoxicated; the building committee divided over the type of facility we needed in order to accommodate current needs and future plans.

Adding to the stress of those two weeks, we'd been understaffed for some time, and regular church ministries seemed to be spinning out of control. One night I wore the hat of the Christian education director; the next, I attended the deacons meeting; then I put on the visionary leader's hat for a building committee meeting; the next night I was at the elders meeting. The routine became crazy—three nights at home in two weeks with one of them spent preparing a sermon. I knew I was in trouble when I discovered myself working six hours on my day off—while still counting it as a day off.

What's a stressed-out pastor to do? How about taking a cue from the apostle Paul, who could see God working in the chaos. For Paul, stress provided an avenue for God's solution. "We were under great pressure, far beyond our ability to endure," he wrote, "but this happened that we might not rely on ourselves but on God" (2 Cor. 1:8-9, NIV). Paul acknowledged being "hard pressed on every side," but he took pains to clarify the fact that in spite of the pressure, he was "not crushed" (2 Cor. 4:8, NIV). Ordinary "jar of clay" that he was, he recognized God's all-surpassing power within (v. 7). He was confident of God's bigger plan; he knew God would guide him through difficulties.

That's why he could write encouraging words for those weighed down by troubles or worries: "Therefore we do not lose heart. Though outwardly we are wasting away, yet inwardly we are being renewed day by day. For our light and momentary troubles are achieving for us an eternal glory that far outweighs them all" (2 Cor. 4:16-17, NIV).

Lightweight. Momentary. Nothing compared to what's coming. It's good to see our problems in the proper perspective.

—Richard Doebler

REFLECTION

When stress threatens to suffocate me, do I focus on my problems? What can I do to concentrate more on God's power that is available to offset the pressures?

PRAYER

Dear God, if tension can create something good in a guitar string, then it's not so much to ask that you use the stress in my life to create something good.

"God promises a safe landing but not a calm passage."

—Bulgarian proverb

52

～ TRANSFORMATION

Lifelong Learner

*Don't copy the behavior and
customs of this world, but let God
transform you into a new person
by changing the way you think.*
ROMANS 12:2

ONE of the best pieces of advice I came by as a young investment banker was from a retired advertising executive who encouraged me to write down in a notebook the names of people I met during my career. I asked to see his notebook, and he showed me forty years' worth of names, notations, addresses, and phone numbers. I remember how impressed I was with his extensive list of business and civic leaders. When I asked why he kept a notebook, he said it was to remind him that his career in advertising was shaped through the people he met. From his notebook he pointed to the names of those who had taught him the meaning of diligence and constancy in one's work. From others, he had learned integrity and fair dealing. No matter the lessons learned, his notebook was a journal of life and the transformational movement that takes place if we are willing to be lifelong learners.

Every other year I commit myself to reading through all the books of the Bible, from Genesis to Revelation. When I read the Bible in its entirety, I am more able to understand the full nature of God rather than focus on an isolated characteristic. In my private study of the Scriptures my tendency is to focus attention on a specific attribute of God, such as love or justice, but I can miss the broader picture of God's wholeness. Each time I read the complete text of the Scriptures, the Word amplifies my understanding of the limitless nature of the Creator.

The Word reveals and informs me of God's boundlessness. And as my knowledge of him grows, I am transformed, sculpted into a closer image of Christ. I am no longer the same person. As my mind ponders the enormousness of God, my heart is impressed by his grace, and my hands are moved to action. Transformational living reflects God's influence in my life as my mind, heart, and hands are harmonized together.

—Dave Sveen

REFLECTION

Am I spending enough time reading God's Word, coming to it with fresh eyes and a teachable spirit, and allowing the Holy Spirit to use the Word to work in me?

PRAYER

Sovereign God, use your Spirit to help me become more like your Son.

"I have never met a soul who has set out to satisfy the Lord and has not been satisfied himself."

—Watchman Nee, twentieth-century Chinese pastor and author

⤸CONTRIBUTORS

David Goetz, compiler, contributor, and general editor, is founder of CustomZines.com, an internet publishing services company based in Wheaton, Illinois. He is former manager of new product development for Christianity Today International and served as associate editor of *Leadership* journal and executive editor of PreachingToday.com. He and his wife, Jana, live in Wheaton with their three children.

⤸

OTHER CONTRIBUTORS

M. Craig Barnes is senior pastor of National Presbyterian Church in Washington, D.C., and the author of *Yearning, When God Interrupts,* and *Hustling God.*

James D. Berkley is senior associate pastor of First Presbyterian Church in Bellevue, Washington. He is a contributing editor to *Leadership* journal and the author of *The Dynamics of Church Finance.*

Richard Nelson Bolles is a vocational counselor and author of the best-selling book *The 1999 What Color Is Your Parachute?* A former pastor, he has also written *How to Find Your Mission in Life* and *How to Create a Picture of Your Ideal Job or Next Career.*

Paul Borden is a consultant for American Baptist Churches of the West in Oakland, California, and also consults internationally, advising churches in Australia and New Zealand. He was a contributor to the *Building Church Leaders Notebook,* PreachingToday.com, and Preaching Today Audio and was also the biblical and theological editor for *Old Testament Foundations* and *New Testament Foundations with Philip Yancey.*

Bob Buford is founder of Leadership Network, an organization that supports innovation and excellence in churches. He is author of *Half-Time: Changing Your Game Plan from Success to Significance.* For many years he was chairman of the board and CEO of Buford Television, Inc., a Texas-based cable TV company.

Richard Doebler is senior pastor of Cloquet Gospel Tabernacle in Cloquet, Minnesota, and is a contributing editor to *Leadership* journal. In addition, he served as an editor for *The Quest Study Bible* as well as *Your Church* and *Computing Today* magazines.

Peter Drucker is founder of the Peter F. Drucker Foundation for Nonprofit Management. He teaches management and social science at the Claremont Graduate School in Claremont, California, and is the author of *The Effective Executive* and *Management Challenges for the 21*st *Century.*

William Easum is founder, president, and senior consultant for 21st Century Strategies, a nonprofit organization devoted to retooling pastors, churches, and denominational leaders for ministry in a new world. He is the author of *Church Growth Handbook* and *How to Reach Baby Boomers.*

Gary Fenton is senior pastor of Dawson Baptist Church in Birmingham, Alabama. A speaker on the subject of leadership and motivation, he is the author of *Your Ministry's Next Chapter* and coauthor of *Mastering Church Finances.*

Mark Galli is editor of *Christian History* magazine and managing editor of *Christianity Today* magazine. He also served as a Presbyterian pastor for ten years in Mexico City and in Sacramento, California. He is coauthor of *Preaching That Connects* and *The Complete Idiot's Guide to Prayer*.

Linda Gehrs is assistant editor for *Men of Integrity*, a men's devotional, *Preaching Today*, a sermon audio series, and *Building Church Leaders Notebook*. Before working for Christianity Today International, she taught English as a foreign language for two years in the Czech Republic and volunteered for six months with Josiah Venture, a mission focusing on youth ministry and leadership development in Eastern Europe.

David Goetz is founder of CustomZines.com and formerly, executive editor of PreachingToday.com. He was also general editor for *Building Church Leaders Notebook* and the Pastor's Soul Series.

Richard C. Halverson (d. 1995) was a former U.S. Senate chaplain and longtime pastor of Fourth Presbyterian Church near Washington, D.C.

Harry J. Heintz is senior pastor of Brunswick Presbyterian Church in Troy, New York, and mentor at Gordon-Conwell Theological Seminary.

Craig Brian Larson is pastor of Lake Shore Church in Chicago, Illinois, and editor of PreachingToday.com and Preaching Today Audio. He is coauthor of *Preaching That Connects*.

Sue Mallory is the executive director of Leadership Training Network, an organization designed to equip and mobilize church leadership, and supporting author of the *Starter Kit for Mobilizing Ministry*. She also founded and was the first president of the Southern California Association for Lay Empowerment and Development.

Steve Mathewson is senior pastor of Dry Creek Bible Church in Belgrade, Montana. He is a contributor to *The Quest Study Bible* and *Building Church Leaders Notebook*. Steve's sermons have been featured on the Preaching Today Audio series.

Kevin A. Miller is vice president of resources for Christianity Today International and editor-at-large of *Leadership* journal. Kevin is the author of *Secrets of Staying Power* and coauthor with his wife, Karen, of *More Than You and Me*.

Mary C. Miller is corporate secretary of the Evangelical Covenant Church. Previously she was pastor of Donaldson Evangelical Covenant Church in Donaldson, Indiana. She is also a contributor to *Leadership* journal.

John Ortberg is a teaching pastor at Willow Creek Community Church and author of *The Life You've Always Wanted* and *Love beyond Reason*.

Earl Palmer is pastor of University Presbyterian Church in Seattle, Washington. He has written a number of books and commentaries, including *Signposts: Christian Values in an Age of Uncertainty* and *Mastering Teaching*.

Ben Patterson is dean of the chapel at Hope College in Holland, Michigan. He previously served Presbyterian (PCUSA) pastorates in New Jersey and California. He is the author of *Waiting: Find Hope When God Seems Silent,* a back-page columnist for *Leadership* journal, and a contributor to *Christianity Today*.

Bob Shank is founder and president of Priority Living, a ministry to business professionals and their families. Before entering vocational ministry, he worked in the construction industry. Bob is the author of *Total Life Management*.

Steve Sjogren is senior pastor of Vineyard Community Church in Cincinnati, Ohio, which is an outreach church with weekend attendance of more than four thousand. A pioneer of servant evangelism, an innovative approach to sharing Christ, he is also the author of *Conspiracy of Kindness* and *Servant Warfare.*

Fred Smith Sr. is an internationally noted author, speaker, and management consultant who has advised and mentored leaders for nearly sixty years. An executive with Genesco for many years, Smith is a contributing editor to *Leadership* journal and a former member of the board of directors of Christianity Today International.

David Sveen is president of the Domanada Foundation, which provides leadership training in Russia and other countries, and of International Sports Ministries in Wheaton, Illinois. He previously spent fifteen years in the field of investment banking, serving as senior vice president and corporate sales manager.

Joni Eareckson Tada is founder of JAF Ministries, a parachurch organization in Agoura Hills, California, that advocates the cause of and ministers to those with disabilities. She is the author of *Heaven* and *More Precious than Silver.*

William Willimon has been dean of the chapel and professor of Christian Ministry at Duke University in Durham, North Carolina, since 1984 and preaches each Sunday in the Duke Chapel. He is the author of forty-three books, including *Sighing for Eden* and *What's Right with the Church.*

Randal C. Working is associate pastor for adult ministries at the First Presbyterian Church of Bellevue, Washington. For several years he worked as a campus minister with Youth for Christ in Switzerland and as an associate pastor in California.

⌇INDEX OF TOPICS

Bold entries indicate the topic under which the devotion appears in the book. Other entries are related topics that the devotion also addresses.

Ambition
  Ambition Crippler 1
  Whatever God Wants 5
Anger
  Anger without Sin 9
Apathy
  Deciding to Decide 13
Attitude
  The Roots of a Joyful Spirit 145
Baptism
  The Myth of Hard Work 85
Beauty
  Hints of Heaven 141
Busyness
  The "God Compartment" 137
Calling
  Leadership Lessons from *The Prince of Egypt* 17
  Have You Been "Discovered"? 65
  Bringing Your Identity to Work 125
Change
  Bringing Your Identity to Work 125
  The Best Is Yet to Come 193
Character
  Beyond the Packaging 21

Unhappy? Maybe That's Good! 25
  Telling Secrets 73
Commitment
  Deciding to Decide 13
  Loving the Game When You're Losing 29
  Everyday Boldness 37
  Stepping into Something Frightening 41
  The "God Compartment" 137
  The Difference between Profit and Prosperity 149
  What's in the Box? 181
Compassion
  True Greatness 121
Confidence
  Ambition Crippler 1
Conflict
  Anger without Sin 9
Contentment
  Have You Been "Discovered"? 65
  Can We Despise God's Grace? 117
Conviction
  One Surpassing Love 153
Courage
  Ambition Crippler 1
  Dashes of Courage 33
  Everyday Boldness 37

Stepping into Something
  Frightening 41
Love Overcomes All Fear
  93
Your Words Came Out
  105
One Surpassing Love 153
The Warehouse with
  Wings 169
Cowardice
  Dashes of Courage 33
Culture
  Sir Paul Goes to the Palace
  133
Cynicism
  The Cynic Within 45
  Cynicism or Realism? 49
Death
  Singled Out 113
Dependence on God
  When God Gives Us a
  Push 97
Desire for God
  The Drink in the Desert
  53
  No Stupid Questions 57
Devotions
  Lifelong Learner 205
Discernment
  Everyday Boldness 37
  Cynicism or Realism? 49
Discipleship
  No Stupid Questions 57
  Feet on Earth, Head in
  Heaven 109
  The Difference between
  Profit and Prosperity 149
  The Best Is Yet to Come
  193
Discontent
  Content with Enough 61
  Have You Been
  "Discovered"? 65
Distrust
  Cynicism or Realism? 49
Doubt
  When Leadership Hurts 81

What You Don't See Can
  Hurt You 177
Dualism
  Sir Paul Goes to the Palace
  133
Ego
  The Unholy Trinity: Me,
  Myself, and I 69
Emotions
  Anger without Sin 9
Empathy
  When Leadership Hurts 81
Eternity
  Hints of Heaven 141
Faithfulness
  Leadership Lessons from
  The Prince of Egypt 17
Fatigue
  Hints of Heaven 141
Fear
  Dashes of Courage 33
  Getting out of the Way 89
  One Surpassing Love 153
  What You Don't See Can
  Hurt You 177
  What's in the Box? 181
Forgiveness
  "I Am What I Am" 185
Free Will
  Can We Change God's
  Mind? 173
Gifts
  Leadership Lessons from
  The Prince of Egypt 17
Glorifying God
  Whatever God Wants 5
Glory
  The Unholy Trinity: Me,
  Myself, and I 69
Goals
  Habit Tracking 189
Goal Setting
  Whatever God Wants 5
Godlessness
  The Cynic Within 45
God's Call
  Ambition Crippler 1

God's Character
  When Leadership Hurts 81
  What Is God Like? 101
  Lifelong Learner 205
God's Discipline
  Telling Secrets 73
God's Faithfulness
  God in the In-Between 77
God's Goodness
  When Leadership Hurts 81
God's Help
  When God Gives Us a
    Push 97
God's Holiness
  What Is God Like? 101
God's Love
  The Myth of Hard Work
    85
  Getting out of the Way 89
  Love Overcomes All Fear
    93
God's Presence
  The Drink in the Desert 53
  God in the In-Between 77
  When God Gives Us a
    Push 97
God's Protection
  Satan's a Bear 197
God's Sovereignty
  What Is God Like? 101
  Singled Out 113
God's Transcendence
  What Is God Like? 101
God's Will
  Can We Change God's
    Mind? 173
God's Word
  Lifelong Learner 205
God's Work in Us
  Your Words Came Out
    105
God's Worthiness
  Feet on Earth, Head in
    Heaven 109
Grace
  The Cynic Within 45
  The Myth of Hard Work
    85

Singled Out 113
  Can We Despise God's
    Grace? 117
  "I Am What I Am" 185
Gratitude
  Can We Despise God's
    Grace? 117
Growth
  The Best Is Yet to Come
    193
Hardships
  The Warehouse with
    Wings 169
Holiness
  Unhappy? Maybe That's
    Good! 25
  Getting out of the Way 89
Holy Spirit
  Your Words Came Out
    105
Honesty
  Never Say Never 129
Honor
  The Unholy Trinity: Me,
    Myself, and I 69
Hope
  The Cynic Within 45
Humility
  Whatever God Wants 5
  Beyond the Packaging 21
  The Unholy Trinity: Me,
    Myself, and I 69
  When God Gives Us a
    Push 97
  What Is God Like? 101
  True Greatness 121
  Never Say Never 129
  What You Don't See Can
    Hurt You 177
Hypocrisy
  Telling Secrets 73
Identity
  Bringing Your Identity to
    Work 125
Integrity
  Beyond the Packaging 21
  Never Say Never 129

217

Sir Paul Goes to the Palace
133

The "God Compartment"
137

Joy
Hints of Heaven 141
The Roots of a Joyful Spirit
145

Leadership
The Warehouse with
Wings 169

Life
Singled Out 113

Longing
The Drink in the Desert 53

Lordship of Christ
The Difference between
Profit and Prosperity 149
What's in the Box? 181

Love
Singled Out 113
True Greatness 121

Love for God
Getting out of the Way 89
One Surpassing Love 153

Marriage
Anger without Sin 9

Martyrdom
One Surpassing Love 153

Materialism
A Tale of Two Tables 157

Meditation
Habit Tracking 189

Mercy
Stepping into Something
Frightening 41
The Myth of Hard Work
85

Ministry
Unhappy? Maybe That's
Good! 25

Motivation
Deciding to Decide 13
Loving the Game When
You're Losing 29
The God Who Perseveres
165

Obedience
Leadership Lessons from
The Prince of Egypt 17
Love Overcomes All Fear
93
Can We Change God's
Mind? 173

Opportunity
Leadership Lessons from
The Prince of Egypt 17

Outreach
Sir Paul Goes to the Palace
133

Pain
When Leadership Hurts 81

Passion
Deciding to Decide 13

Peace
Greater Than Our
Accomplishments 161

Perseverance
Everyday Boldness 37
God in the In-Between 77
The God Who Perseveres
165
The Warehouse with
Wings 169

Persistence
Can We Change God's
Mind? 173

Perspective
The Cynic Within 45
God in the In-Between 77
An Unseen Enemy 201

Poverty
A Tale of Two Tables 157

Prayer
No Stupid Questions 57
When God Gives Us a
Push 97
Can We Change God's
Mind? 173
Habit Tracking 189
Satan's a Bear 197

Pride
Whatever God Wants 5
True Greatness 121

What You Don't See Can
  Hurt You 177
Priorities
  Getting out of the Way 89
  A Tale of Two Tables 157
  What's in the Box? 181
  Habit Tracking 189
Prisons
  Stepping into Something
    Frightening 41
Purity of Heart
  Beyond the Packaging 21
  No Stupid Questions 57
  The "God Compartment"
    137
Purpose
  What's in the Box? 181
Risk
  Everyday Boldness 37
  Love Overcomes All Fear
    93
Sacrifice
  Feet on Earth, Head in
    Heaven 109
  Singled Out 113
Salvation
  The Myth of Hard Work
    85
  Singled Out 113
Sanctification
  Unhappy? Maybe That's
    Good! 25
Satisfaction
  The Drink in the Desert 53
  Have You Been
    "Discovered"? 65
Seeking God
  No Stupid Questions 57
Self-Acceptance
  "I Am What I Am" 185
Self-Concept
  The Unholy Trinity: Me,
    Myself, and I 69
Self-Doubt
  "I Am What I Am" 185
Self-Esteem
  The Unholy Trinity: Me,
    Myself, and I 69

Bringing Your Identity to
  Work 125
Self-Examination
  Telling Secrets 73
Self-Fulfillment
  The "God Compartment"
    137
Self-Inventory
  Habit Tracking 189
Selfish Ambition
  Content with Enough 61
Servanthood
  True Greatness 121
Service
  Unhappy? Maybe That's
    Good! 25
  Stepping into Something
    Frightening 41
  Feet on Earth, Head in
    Heaven 109
Setbacks
  The Warehouse with
    Wings 169
Simplicity
  True Greatness 121
Sin
  Anger without Sin 9
  Telling Secrets 73
  "I Am What I Am" 185
Sincerity
  Beyond the Packaging 21
Social Justice
  Stepping into Something
    Frightening 41
Sophistication
  True Greatness 121
Sorrow
  The Roots of a Joyful Spirit
    145
Spiritual Disciplines
  Lifelong Learner 205
Spiritual Health
  The Roots of a Joyful Spirit
    145
Spiritual Maturity
  The Best Is Yet to Come
    193

219

Spiritual Warfare
  Satan's a Bear 197
  An Unseen Enemy 201
Stewardship
  A Tale of Two Tables 157
Stress
  The God Who Perseveres
    165
  An Unseen Enemy 201
Success
  Loving the Game When
    You're Losing 29
  Greater Than Our
    Accomplishments 161
Suffering
  When Leadership Hurts 81
  Feet on Earth, Head in
    Heaven 109
  The God Who Perseveres
    165
  The Warehouse with
    Wings 169
  The Best Is Yet to Come
    193
  Satan's a Bear 197
Support
  Your Words Came Out
    105
Surrender
  The Difference between
    Profit and Prosperity 149
Temptation
  Content with Enough 61
  Never Say Never 129
  The Roots of a Joyful Spirit
    145
Thankfulness
  Hints of Heaven 141

The Ordinary
  God in the In-Between 77
Transformation
  Ambition Crippler 1
  Lifelong Learner 205
Trust
  Deciding to Decide 13
  The Difference between
    Profit and Prosperity 149
  Greater Than Our
    Accomplishments 161
  The God Who Perseveres
    165
  Satan's a Bear 197
Truth
  Dashes of Courage 33
Vulnerability
  Never Say Never 129
Wealth
  A Tale of Two Tables 157
Weariness
  Hints of Heaven 141
Witnessing
  Dashes of Courage 33
  Sir Paul Goes to the Palace
    133
  One Surpassing Love 153
Work
  Bringing Your Identity to
    Work 125
Works
  The Myth of Hard Work
    85
Worship
  Your Words Came Out
    105

Index of
Scripture References

OLD TESTAMENT

Genesis 3:3   61
Exodus 4:1-2   17
Exodus 4:13   1
Exodus 33:19; 34:6-7   81
1 Samuel 30:6   73
2 Samuel 6:16   49
2 Samuel 12: 8-10   117
Nehemiah 2:4-5   37
Psalm 51:17   69
Psalm 8:3-4   141
Psalm 23:1-3   89
Psalm 42:1   53
Psalm 46:10-11   161
Psalm 56:1-2   169
Psalm 62:1-2   125
Psalm 91:9-11   33
Psalm 139:23-24   189
Psalm 143:10   77
Proverbs 15:17   157
Proverbs 29:11, 22   9
Ecclesiastes 1:8   45
Isaiah 40:10-12   97
Isaiah 55:8-9   101
Jeremiah 29:11   193

NEW TESTAMENT

Matthew 3:17   85
Matthew 6:33   149
Matthew 10:37-39   153
Matthew 23:12   177
Matthew 25:44-46   41
Mark 7:25   173
John 1:38   57
John 15:11   145
John 20:15-16   113
Romans 12:2   205
1 Corinthians 10:12   129
1 Corinthians 13:1   121
1 Corinthians 15:8-10   185
2 Corinthians 1:8   201
2 Corinthians 6:4-6   109
2 Corinthians 10:10; 11:6   21
Ephesians 1:4   25
Ephesians 3:20-21   133
Ephesians 6:10   29
Philippians 3:7-8   5
Philippians 4:4-7   13
Philippians 4:13   105
Colossians 1:17   137
Colossians 1:17-18   181
1 Timothy 6:12   65
James 1:2-3   165
1 Peter 5:6-9   197
1 John 4:16-18   93

≈APPENDIX

The following is a list of sources in which previously published devotionals appeared.

"Whatever God Wants" by Richard Nelson Bolles is based on material previously published in *Leadership* journal under the title "The Pastor's Parachute," summer 1990, by Christianity Today International.

"Anger without Sin" by John Ortberg was adapted from *Dangers, Toils and Snares,* published in 1994 by Christianity Today International.

"Beyond the Packaging" by Joni Eareckson Tada is based on material previously published in *Leadership* journal - under the title "Thriving with Limitations," winter 1996, by Christianity Today International.

"Feet on Earth, Head in Heaven" by Ben Patterson was taken from *Deepening Your Conversation with God,* published in 1999 by Bethany House Publishers.

"Bringing Your Identity to Work" by Bob Shank is based on material previously published in *Leadership* journal - under the title "Helping the Successful Become Significant," winter 1996, by Christianity Today International.

"Hints of Heaven" by Linda Gehrs is based on material previously published in the Church Leaders Online newsletter under the title "Hints of Heaven: A Taste of

Our Life to Come," April 21, 1999, by Christianity Online.

"Greater than Our Accomplishments" by Fred Smith Sr. was taken from *Leading with Integrity,* published in 1999 by Bethany House Publishers.

"Can We Change God's Mind?" by Ben Patterson was taken from *Deepening Your Conversation with God,* published in 1999 by Bethany House Publishers.

"I Am What I Am" by Richard C. Halverson is based on material previously published in *Leadership* journal - under the title "Planting Seeds and Watching Them Grow," fall 1980, by Christianity Today International.

"Habit Tracking" by Peter Drucker is based on material previously published in *Leadership* journal under the title "Managing to Minister," spring 1989, by Christianity Today International.

LEADERSHIP RESOURCES FROM TYNDALE HOUSE PUBLISHERS, INC.

Jesus on Leadership by C. Gene Wilkes: Seven principles of leadership based on Christ's example

Leadership Prayers by Richard Kriegbaum: Prayers and reflections on being an effective leader

Leadership Devotions compiled by David Goetz: Fifty-two devotions focusing on building the internal character of Christian leaders

Leadership Meditations compiled by David Goetz: Fifty-two meditations focusing on the external aspects of leadership

ADDITIONAL MATERIALS FROM LEADERSHIP RESOURCES

Preaching Today Online
This Web site offers paid subscribers access to weekly illustrations for preaching, practical journal articles, and a searchable database for illustrations and quotations. For more information, visit www.preachingtoday.com.

Preaching Today Audio
Subscribers receive monthly two sermons and one workshop on preaching from teachers such as Bill Hybels and Haddon Robinson as well as printed sermon transcripts. To subscribe, call 1-800-806-7796.

Building Church Leaders Notebook
Provides twelve timely themes from which pastors can train their church leaders. Each chapter includes an interview with a respected church leader, practical assessment tools, case studies, and devotionals. To order, call 1-800-806-7798.

Building Church Leaders Quarterly
Provides subscribers with training materials for those in church leadership. New themes begin every three months. Included with each theme is a softcover book containing interviews, performance assessments, case studies, devotionals, and other activities. To subscribe, call 1-800-806-7796.

Leadership Resources is a division of Christianity Today International.

Leadership®